Ann Oakley works at the National Perinatal Epidemiology Unit, Radcliffe Infirmary, Oxford. She is a feminist writer, researcher, sociologist and mother, and author of a number of books on gender roles and the position of women, including *Women Confined* (1980), *Subject Women* (1981, also in Fontana) and her autobiography, *Taking it Like a Woman* (1984). She lives in London with her three children.

Ann McPherson is a General Practitioner in Oxford, with a special interest in women's health problems. Her previous books include *Mum, I Feel Funny: a Family Guide to Common Ailments* (with A. Macfarlane and N. Garland, 1982) and *Women's Problems in General Practice* (ed., with Ann Anderson, 1983). She is married with three children.

Helen Roberts is Senior Researcher at Bradford and Ilkley Community College. Her previous books include *Doing Feminist Research* (ed., 1981) and *Women, Health and Reproduction* (ed., 1981), and she has written numerous articles on women's issues. She has a baby son and is stepmother to three teenagers.

Miscarriage

Ann Oakley, Ann McPherson
and Helen Roberts

Fontana Paperbacks

First published by Fontana Paperbacks 1984

Copyright © Ann Oakley, Ann McPherson
and Helen Roberts 1984

Set in Linotron Plantin

Made and printed in Great Britain by
William Collins Sons & Co. Ltd, Glasgow

Grateful acknowledgment is made to Olwyn Hughes
for permission to reproduce the extract from
'Three Women: a Poem for Three Voices' by
Sylvia Plath (*Winter Trees*, 1971).

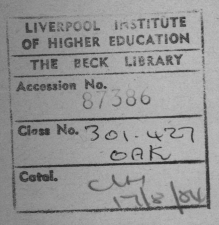

Contents

List of Figures

I am not ugly. I am even beautiful.
The mirror gives back a woman without deformity.
The nurses give back my clothes, and an identity.
It is usual, they say, for such a thing to happen.
It is usual in my life, and the lives of others.
I am one in five, something like that. I am not hopeless.
I am beautiful as a statistic. Here is my lipstick.

I draw on the old mouth.
The red mouth I put by with my identity
A day ago, two days, three days ago. It was a Friday.
I do not even need a holiday; I can go to work today.
I can love my husband, who will understand.
Who will love me through the blur of my deformity,
As if I had lost an eye, a leg, a tongue.

And so I stand, a little sightless. So I walk
Away on wheels, instead of legs, they serve me well.
And learn to speak with fingers, not a tongue.
The body is resourceful.
The body of a starfish can grow back its arms.
And newts are prodigal in legs. And may I be
As prodigal in what lacks me.

From 'Three Women: a Poem for Three Voices'
by Sylvia Plath

Introduction

This book is the outcome of a joint effort. It was produced with great commitment but also considerable difficulty from the interstices of three lives occupied with three jobs and seven children and lived in three different places. We have tried to be exhaustive in our research of the literature, and this, in itself, has led us to realize the surprising lack of information that there is, especially in the areas of women's emotional reactions to miscarriage, and as to what is considered appropriate treatment by the professionals. Because of this, we are only too aware of the book's potential shortcomings. Nevertheless, even with this shortage of knowledge, it seemed to us important simply to get on and produce the book, so that women having miscarriages and those providing care for them would have a readily available source of information.

We have written the book as professionals with an interest in this field – two medical sociologists and one general practitioner – but also, first and foremost, as women. To our (collective) seven children we would add five miscarriages – not, as we emphasize in this book, an unusual number, but really very much an integral part of women's reproductive experience, although a hidden part in a society unable easily to confront such basic issues of life and death.

Many people have helped us with the book. We would especially like to thank the late Anne Anderson, as well as Martin Bobrow, Iain Chalmers, Juliet Cheetham, Angela Coulter, Diana Elbourne, Robert Harrison, Michael Irwin, Aidan Macfarlane, Alison Macfarlane, Ian MacKenzie, Klim McPherson, Rachel Miller, Miranda Mugford, Robin Oakley, Jessie Parfit, Chris Redman and Julian Wolfson.

11

Although we have benefited from their help and advice, the final form of the book is, of course, our responsibility alone. We are indebted to Jini Hetherington, Lesley Mierh, Sue Sinclair and Sheila Woodley for secretarial help, and particularly for deciphering three often illegible forms of handwriting. We are grateful to all the women who carefully and in great detail filled in the questionnaires we made available through *Mother and Baby* magazine, and through the newsletter of the National Association of the Childless, or who simply sent us accounts of their miscarriages when they heard we were writing this book. These women are really co-authors of the book, since their accounts of, and comments on, the experience of miscarriage appear throughout it. We note how many of them thanked us at the bottom of their questionnaires for 'listening' to them, and hope they feel that in the resulting book we have indeed succeeded in listening to them. As a courtesy to them, their families and friends, we have not used their real names in the text. Although we have used material from these questionnaires throughout the book, we have reserved discussion of the survey for appendix I. We would also like to thank all the doctors who responded so helpfully to our questions about their treatment of, and attitudes towards, miscarriage, and whose answers are included in chapter 9.

Miscarriage is the first British book of its kind on the subject. We hope that the book will be useful to the many women in Britain and elsewhere who undergo miscarriage and who, in the aftermath of what is often a totally unexpected event, find a need for information and the sharing of experience. We calculate that, taking the most conservative estimate of the incidence of miscarriage, there are at least 426,000 miscarriages annually in Britain (as compared with around 640,000 births). Professionals who come into contact with women having miscarriages do not always have the time to give information, or to 'talk through' the experience. We hope they will also appreciate the book, and refer their clients to it.

Although this is the first British book of its kind dealing

with miscarriage, the causes and consequences of miscarriage have puzzled women and the professionals who care for them for centuries. We think it appropriate to end this introduction by quoting the words of one Augustus Bozzi Granville, who was Physician-Accoucheur to the Westminster General Dispensary in London in 1818. Granville did his own 'mini-survey' of miscarriages among women attending the Dispensary in that year, and discovered that the first 400 he asked had experienced 305 miscarriages between them. He found they remembered these events 'with a tenacity that nothing can relax', and commented that, although he was impressed by the frequency of miscarriage, he was also impressed by the fact that 'the unpleasant consequences of abortion [miscarriage], even where it has occurred repeatedly in the same individual, appear to have been few, and those, comparatively speaking, of no great importance – and not particularly influencing the exercise of those functions which essentially characterize the female sex'. The point Granville was making is that good health and successful pregnancy are likely even after many miscarriages. But this says nothing about the emotional and social impact of miscarriage, which may be profound. It is this contradiction between a common, and relatively unimportant physical happening, on the one hand, and an event of often major emotional proportions on the other, that forms the central theme of our book.

1 The Meaning of Miscarriage

Until I miscarried I had no idea how common an occurrence it is. I feel that the whole subject should be more publicized to increase our understanding of the subject. I also feel that some medical and nursing staff have a rather blasé attitude about it, and tend to underestimate the emotional after-effects of miscarriage. The general attitude seems to be 'you'll soon get over it, and you're young enough to try again' – almost as if the lost baby was never conceived and didn't matter.

Miscarriage is a very common event. As many as three-quarters of all human conceptions do not result in the birth at full term of a live baby, but are lost at some stage in pregnancy. World-wide, around one million women become pregnant every day. At least half these pregnancies end in miscarriage or stillbirth, 15 per cent are deliberately aborted, and of the children born, a further 10 per cent die in their first year. What we call 'miscarriage' is therefore really one aspect of a whole spectrum of reproductive loss, and pregnancy loss is a normal part of human existence – biologically speaking, of course. Most of these miscarriages take place before 10–12 weeks of pregnancy.

There have been various estimates as to the true incidence of miscarriage. The figures arrived at go from one in six of all pregnancies miscarried, to four out of six. Studies asking about, and looking back over women's pregnancy histories, produce lower rates of miscarriage than those in which women trying to become pregnant are studied carefully for signs of conception and early pregnancy loss. The figure also depends on when one takes a pregnancy to have started. If pregnancy is diagnosed by when the first period is missed and the woman feels she is pregnant, then there will be fewer miscarriages than if pregnancy is taken to start the moment the egg and sperm meet and join. If one takes implantation into the wall of the uterus as the time the pregnancy starts, then the figure for the incidence of miscarriage will be somewhere between the two. In one recent study 197 volunteer women wishing to conceive were followed and their urine was tested using a very sensitive method of pregnancy testing which could diagnose pregnancy very early after conception. One hundred and fifty-two pregnancies were diagnosed using biochemical tests, but 43 per cent of these had miscarried by the twentieth week of pregnancy. Interestingly, only a minority of these women ever 'knew' they were pregnant – the miscarriage happened so early for many of them that there had been no obvious physical evidence of pregnancy. Using this sort of data we could say that, since the size of the average family is 2.4 – in other words 'most' women have between two and three children, it could well be the case that half these women have actually experienced a miscarriage of which they are not aware.

Many women do not talk about their miscarriages, for to admit that one has not been able to sustain a pregnancy for long enough to give birth to a baby may be regarded as shameful, even in these days of women's 'liberation'. Occasionally a newsworthy miscarriage hits the headlines: thus the *Sun* in April 1983 carried the headline 'Baby Agony of Snooker Champ'. It was not the snooker champ's (Cliff Thorburn) own agony, but that of his wife Barbara, who miscarried at ten weeks in Canada while Thorburn was playing world championship snooker in Sheffield. Fame rendered the event publicly important, but most miscarriages have a significance to the women and men concerned that is no less great for being of an intensely private nature.

Miscarriage, like other physical experiences such as the common cold, may happen often, but this does not mean that we necessarily understand a great deal about it. Indeed, the causes of miscarriage are quite poorly understood. We are not even sure what kind of treatment women get after miscarriage, or which forms of treatment are really effective. Some of this lack of knowledge may be due to the very frequency with which miscarriage occurs: to doctors it may appear as a routine event not worth taking terribly seriously. After all, even with three miscarriages behind her, a woman stands at least a 60 per cent chance of having a healthy baby in the next pregnancy. In addition, from the point of view of doctors' own work satisfaction, a miscarriage has, of course, less of the excitement and satisfaction of the birth of a live baby.

But to women themselves a miscarriage is rarely a trivial event. That is why we have written this book. For most women the experience and consequences of miscarriage are not easily forgotten. There may be aspects of the experience which jar for a long time, and questions about it that are not answered and sometimes not asked. Another reason for writing the book is that, apart from medical textbooks, there is very little available literature on the experience of miscarriage. If you go along to your local library or bookshop you will find many books about pregnancy and childbirth, but only one or two about miscarriage. Even women's health handbooks tend not to devote much space to miscarriage.

Our aims in this book are therefore to:

– provide an accurate and up-to-date guide as to what is medically known about the symptoms, causes, treatments and consequences of miscarriage;
– take account both of the reality and the diversity of women's experiences of miscarriage;
– consider not only physical but emotional aspects of the experience;
– answer the detailed and practical questions women have during or after miscarriage and which they cannot easily get answered from other sources.

Many of the questions we discuss are relevant not only to

17

miscarriage but to all such kinds of loss, including stillbirth, and the death of a very young baby. We have chosen, however, to focus specifically on miscarriage – that is the loss of fetuses too young and immature to have a chance of survival. (A few of the women whose experiences we draw on gave birth to fetuses who lived for a few minutes or hours, but these are the exception.) We have focused on miscarriage because we believe that the topics of stillbirth and perinatal death are somewhat better covered than miscarriage. There is more awareness of the sensitive and personal nature of these events in books on pregnancy and childbirth and among doctors. By comparison, miscarriage is a topic which is still spoken about in hushed tones, or not at all.

The book will deal with the lived experiences – which are often left out as being too 'subjective' to take seriously – as well as with such medical advice and information as is available. An important consideration in writing the book is to help fill in the information gaps that some GPs and specialist obstetricians/gynaecologists either do not have the time to go into in detail when talking to their patients or are not particularly interested in providing. What are the chances of having a second miscarriage? How soon should one try again? Is there anything a woman can do to lower her chances of having another miscarriage? These are the sorts of questions we hope to answer both for women embarking on pregnancies, women who have had miscarriages, and the professionals who see these women.

Medical terms used to describe miscarriage

We need, first of all, to define what a miscarriage is. A miscarriage, meaning 'the expulsion of a fetus from the womb before 28 weeks of pregnancy', is the popular term for what in medical circles is called a spontaneous abortion. 'Miscarriage' is the older word – 'abortion' did not start to come into common use until the late seventeenth century. In medical terminology 'spontaneous abortion' is contrasted with 'induced abortion' – the deliberate termination of a pregnancy, or what most people call, simply, an abortion. Some other terms you might hear in this context, and which we will discuss in this book, are:

Threatened abortion This means bleeding or spotting from the vagina during the first 28 weeks of pregnancy, usually not accompanied by pain, although there may be minor cramps. A threatened abortion suggests that the pregnancy might be in danger, but many women who have bleeding in early pregnancy do go on to have healthy babies (see pages 167–9).

Inevitable abortion Loss of the baby becomes inevitable when the bleeding increases and the pain becomes more intense. The cervix (neck of the womb) opens and eventually the fetus is expelled.

Complete abortion This means that the miscarriage is over and all of what are medically referred to as 'the products of conception' (fetus, amniotic sac and placenta) have come away.

Incomplete abortion The miscarriage is not complete – some of the products of conception remain in the uterus with the consequence that bleeding usually continues and the symptoms of miscarriage do not go away.

Missed abortion In this type of miscarriage the fetus has failed to develop properly or has developed and then died, but is not immediately lost. Many signs of pregnancy (such as breast tenderness and nausea) disappear. One does not have a period, but there may be some spotting of blood. Eventually a spontaneous miscarriage can occur, but if it doesn't a D & C (dilation and curettage) or vacuum aspiration is necessary (see pages 90–2).

Habitual (sometimes called *recurrent*) *abortion* Miscarriage has literally become a 'habit' – it occurs on three or more consecutive occasions.

Septic abortion Infection of the womb may occur with any miscarriage or abortion but usually occurs when the miscarriage is incomplete.

Hydatidiform mole This is a pregnancy in which the placenta develops abnormally and in which (usually) no fetus is present. The placenta grows into a mass of fluid-filled sacs resembling a bunch of grapes. Hydatidiform mole is a rare complication of pregnancy – it occurs in about 1 in 2000 pregnancies in Western countries. With a molar pregnancy the early signs of pregnancy are normal but bleeding starts sooner or later. There may be severe nausea and vomiting due to the high hormone levels caused by the excessive placental growth, and the uterus may enlarge more rapidly than usual. Some moles will miscarry spontaneously, but otherwise a D & C or vacuum aspiration is necessary (and should be done even when the mole has spontaneously miscarried to make sure the uterus is completely empty). It is necessary to have frequent checkups after a molar pregnancy because in some cases (about 10 per cent) a rare form of cancer called choriocarcinoma may develop. With modern forms of treatment this is nearly 100 per cent curable. Because of this risk, women are usually advised not to get pregnant for about a year after a molar pregnancy.

It is probably no accident that when women talk about the spontaneous loss of a pregnancy, they tend to use the lay term miscarriage, reserving 'abortion' for a pregnancy that is ended deliberately. Although clinically the two experiences may be classified under the same heading, they are not at all the same to the women undergoing them:

> I wish the medical term 'abortion' wouldn't be used when it is a natural miscarriage. I found that very upsetting as I felt that I had in some way killed the baby.

Looking back on it, one thing that upset me out of all proportion was that on my medical certificate the doctor put 'abortion' and not miscarriage. I know they are one and the same and that abortion is a medical term for early miscarriage, but to me at that time abortion meant to take a decision to end a pregnancy.

I think I probably felt that losing the baby was my fault, and the word 'abortion' seemed to confirm that.

This woman was so upset that her mother eventually persuaded the doctor to change the term on the medical certificate.

The variety of miscarriage experiences

Within the framework of these definitions, women's experiences may be quite diverse. A social worker aged 31 describes losing her first pregnancy:

I initially had one or two brown spots, I went to the doctor who said I may have broken a blood vessel. Over 24 hours, the loss increased . . . Next morning I had a heavy loss and immediately called the doctor who came very quickly. He advised bed rest and said I was threatening to miscarry. After lunch I started to get cramps and increased bleeding. At about 4.30 I felt I needed to go to the loo, where I lost the baby.

I felt very sad initially but then hopeful for the next pregnancy and accepting that there may have been something wrong with the baby . . . it may have been 'for the best'.

This experience was over quite quickly, the woman was not hospitalized, and was able to take some comfort from the thought that it could have been 'for the best' (she went on to have a normal full-term baby almost exactly a year after the miscarriage). By contrast, Valerie Kingston lost her baby in hospital later in pregnancy:

> I felt the baby moving low down, and noticed a slight loss of fluid . . . this went on for two or three days until I noticed some blood. This prompted me to consult my doctor, who had me admitted to hospital, as it was suspected the membranes had ruptured. That night I lost a flood of blood and fluid, but it was not decided that I had lost the baby until the cord came down (two days later) and the doctor said it had stopped pulsating. I was then put on a drip to induce contractions, and seven and a half hours later the baby was delivered. Only one nurse was with me; she did her best not to let me see, but I couldn't help looking at the tiny limp body which was my baby.
>
> I was devastated. I had a happy, healthy pregnancy previously. Everything happened so quickly it was a terrible shock.

Women's reactions to miscarriage vary according to the time in pregnancy when the miscarriage occurs, according to their previous experiences (whether or not they have had problem pregnancies before) and according to their emotional investment in this particular pregnancy. Sally Baines, a voluntary worker, who miscarried at seven weeks in her first pregnancy after a lengthy period of infertility, found a positive side to miscarriage:

> Having been trying for a baby for a considerable time, I was of the attitude that at least I could become pregnant – and was relieved that it ended after having felt ill for three weeks. I was worried that if the pregnancy continued after having had so much pain the baby may have not developed correctly.

By contrast, the mother of two, a university research assistant, described her miscarriage at eleven weeks as a terrible experience – in part, it seems, because having had two normal pregnancies, the idea of miscarriage never crossed her mind beforehand. This woman described her reactions thus:

> [I feel] very frustrated at not knowing *exactly* what caused it. Also 'why me?' An unbearable feeling when hearing of friends' new babies which still makes me physically sick and ill. I feel what a waste of what I'm sure was a perfect baby which was so wanted. A feeling of shame at not being able to produce a baby . . .

Suzanne Matcheson had the added complication of having told her two children, then aged seven and five, about the expected baby: they had been thrilled and had told everyone at school. Four months after the event:

> My confidence was *completely* gone in regard to procreation, yet I crave a third baby as we always intended to have three children. I feel I would be so anxious now in another pregnancy – that the same thing would happen again – that it probably would . . . I . . . now am frankly frightened of the whole process as it has been such a shock to my whole system. In fact, the worst experience of my life . . .

There are no general rules which apply to everyone's reactions to miscarriage, and two women with similar histories and backgrounds miscarrying at the same point in pregnancy may differ radically from one another in their reactions. Having a series of miscarriages, a woman can also find herself in the midst of a series of somewhat differing reactions. Thus a social worker, who had four miscarriages at 12, 8, 16 and 12 weeks, put her reactions in the following terms:

First miscarriage.	Confused.
Second miscarriage.	Perplexed, sad, disappointed.
Third miscarriage.	Grief-stricken, empty, angry, bewildered, cheated, let down.

Fourth miscarriage. Sad, relieved to have D & C,* disappointed, numb.

Women's feelings following miscarriage can be affected by their knowledge of the reasons for their miscarriages. Rowena Carter first lost a pregnancy at seven weeks in 1979 and felt 'desperately unhappy . . . convinced something was wrong with me'. Fourteen months later in 1980 she had a baby and then eighteen months after that at the beginning of 1982 another miscarriage of an unplanned pregnancy complicated by the presence of a coil in the womb:

I bled for about three or four weeks and then lost it. It wasn't as bad as the first time, and I never saw the doctor as it didn't really seem worth it.

The third miscarriage of a planned pregnancy was six months later and Rowena described her response as:

A mixture. Depressed, miserable and confused. In the end, after twelve weeks, I was relieved to get it over with, though I was very depressed.

Although we say there are no general rules for predicting the emotional aftermath of miscarriage, there are a few themes which crop up again and again in the accounts women sent us. The first and most dominant is what could be called the 'why me?' syndrome – the urge to make sense of the experience, to settle on an explanation as to why it happened. We write about this in chapter 5. Another recurrent theme is the impact of the medical management of the miscarriage on subsequent emotional adjustment, a theme well-illustrated in Mary Elgar's description of what happened to her:

Although it is only two weeks ago, I feel really good. I

---

* See pages 91–2

spent the two days after the miscarriage cooking, baking, cleaning, anything so I wouldn't cry and get depressed. I felt incredibly empty and disappointed and still do when I think of it. I feel, though, that the way I was treated helped me recover quickly. In hospital, the nurses were so kind and the SEN who was with me when I actually miscarried was a girl I'd known during nurses' training. There were staff on the ward that I knew from when I'd worked there as a student nurse eight years ago. One patient across from me was really kind, talked to me and ran to get the nurse when I really bled.

It isn't only the attitude of staff and co-patients that can affect women's emotional equilibrium. Another popular theme is the power of social attitudes to mould post-miscarriage adjustment: 'My mother-in-law accused me of making her son worry and if her dog could do it, what was wrong with me?' Or, less directly, but nonetheless hurtfully,

This is a matter which people will discuss less than cancer or death. Each time, those who knew said, 'Better luck next time', and you are left alone to suffer your bereavement . . .

Friends, and colleagues (social workers at that!) were embarrassed to the point of avoiding me. I desperately needed to acknowledge what had happened to me and openly grieve but people wouldn't allow me to. The only person who openly comforted me was the husband of a girl who had also recently suffered a miscarriage. (Social worker, whose account of miscarriage is on page 21.)

An underlying motif here is the irreplaceability of one fetus or baby by another:

I just wish people would not come out with 'Never mind, you're both young, you can have another'! People just don't understand that you don't care about any more you can have, you want the one you've just lost. Although I have a lovely baby boy, I still wonder what the first one would have been . . .

For those of us who must continue to live with the event of miscarriage without the comfort of a successful pregnancy, there is the added stigma of childlessness with which to contend. In the words of Janice Jackson for whom the silence surrounding miscarriage is more complete than that surrounding cancer or death,

We are treated in a strange way because we are childless. Many imply that we never wanted children . . .

My lasting pain will be the attitude of my mother who died at Christmas. She always maintained she saw no point in marriage without children. I failed in trying to explain to her how it is not to be able to have children.

Legal definitions of live- and stillbirth

Because of the need to collect accurate statistics, and because of legal requirements, it is necessary to have clear definitions of what is meant by the actual terms 'miscarriage', 'abortion', 'livebirth' and 'stillbirth'. Not surprisingly, this rather technical framework of medical terminology and legal definitions cannot take into account the very wide variety of delicate shadings of women's different experiences of miscarriage. For example, a miscarriage may occur up to 28 weeks of pregnancy and the experience may be much closer to a 'real' birth. Nevertheless, up to 28 weeks, a dead fetus, however much it may be a baby to the parents, has no legal status, does not have to be registered as a birth or a death, or indeed be buried. From 28 weeks, if a child is born and shows no sign of life, it is deemed to have been stillborn; it has to be registered, and the body properly disposed of, though this may be done by the hospital.

Legal definitions of what constitutes a miscarriage have

Table 1.1   Definitions of live- and stillbirths in force in the United Kingdom

	England and Wales	Scotland	Northern Ireland
Definitions			
Birth	'Birth means a live birth or a stillbirth'	'Birth includes a stillbirth'	'Birth means a live birth or a stillbirth'
Livebirth	'Livebirth means a child born alive'	'No explicit definition'	'Livebirth means a child born alive'
Stillbirth	A stillborn child is 'a child which has issued forth from its mother after the 28th week of pregnancy and which did not at any time after being completely expelled from its mother breathe or show any other signs of life'.	A stillborn child is 'a child which has issued forth from its mother after the 28th week of pregnancy and which did not at any time after being completely expelled from its mother breathe or show any other signs of life'.	A stillbirth 'means the complete expulsion from its mother after the 28th week of pregnancy of a child which did not at any time after being completely expelled or extracted breathe or show any other evidence of life'.
Time within which event is required to be registered			
Birth	42 days	21 days	42 days
Death	5 days	8 days	5 days

Source: Macfarlane and Mugford, 1984

changed over the years, and vary from one country to another. We have put in table 1.1 the definitions of live- and stillbirth currently in force in the UK, together with the time within which births and deaths are required by law to be registered. Developments in medical practice alter the relevance of these legal definitions from time to time. Thus, at the moment, in Britain and other countries with sophisticated obstetric and paediatric services, the higher survival rates of babies born between 23 and 28 weeks of pregnancy are now challenging the legal definition of 28 weeks as the dividing line between death and survival. In 1960, 61 per cent of babies born weighing 1500 g (3 lb 6 oz) or under were born alive, compared with 78 per cent in 1981. Of those very low birthweight babies born in 1960, 33 per cent were still alive at the end of the first month of life, but this figure has more than doubled, becoming 68 per cent by 1981. What this means is that a small baby born at, say, 27 weeks, now has a much higher chance of living than twenty years ago. The mother of such an infant in 1960 may thus have thought of herself as having a miscarriage, whereas the same mother in 1980 may emerge from the trauma of pre-term delivery with a live and healthy baby.

Living with the past

When women recall their experiences of miscarriage, they often do so with great clarity and in minute detail, even if the experience happened some years previously. It is characteristic of these recollections that there is attention to small details, memories of conversations, a reliving of the physical symptoms of miscarriage, and that all these different components of the recollection are combined at the same time with the description of emotional reactions to the event. In describing her emotional reactions every woman is pursuing the meaning of the event for her – given her own attitudes to children, her own family circumstances, her own aspirations for herself as a woman, and her relationship with

her own body. As many of the women who filled in our
questionnaire wrote, a miscarriage is rarely merely forgotten:
rather, over a period of time women learn to accept the loss
and live with it as a part of life. Many factors are involved
in this long-term emotional accommodation to the fact of
miscarriage, including the opportunity to talk about the
meaning of what happened and reliving the experience in
dreams, where fears may sometimes be more readily
expressed. (Of course we are aware that such reactions are
probably over-represented in our survey, and women who
accepted miscarriage more easily were much less likely to
write to us. But the point about the *process* of adjusting to
miscarriage is the same for both groups.)

We end this chapter with Carole Saunder's description of
what happened to her in the course of two pregnancies, one
that miscarried around 22 weeks, and one that resulted in the
birth of live, healthy twins at 33 weeks. In her recollections
some general features of the experience of miscarriage are
clear: the powerful impact on one's mental state of
sympathetic or unsympathetic medical staff, the supreme
difficulty of losing a baby in a society where only the positive
characteristics of motherhood are stressed, the need to
grieve, the blurring of dreams and reality in the months
following miscarriage. Carole only really came to terms with
her miscarriage some eighteen months later, when her twins
were seven months old.

First pregnancy:

I will always remember that last week. I had begun to feel
unwell, nothing specific. Since the beginning, I had had
uterine cramps ('nothing to worry about, it's only your
uterus expanding') and they were becoming more
frequent. On that Wednesday evening, I went to the
library, but left early as I felt so unwell. As I walked home
on that peaceful September evening, a thought so
unexpected it was almost audible popped into my head, 'I
am going to miscarry tonight.' I went to bed and slept

soundly until 9 p.m. when the pain of the cramps woke me, and I felt painfully constipated. When I went to the lavatory, the waters ruptured with a single bright red spot of blood. My husband was not due home until midnight and I was alone.

By the time I reached hospital, I was bleeding profusely, and in casualty they removed the fetus with forceps. I couldn't stop talking and strangely felt no pain till afterwards. The casualty doctor was good and he showed me the small, pink, perfect and still fetus, which I will always be grateful for. Over and over, I cursed myself for not asking what sex it was, even calling it 'it' seems to diminish the reality. It is like trying to mourn something abstract, something that existed in the imagination . . . I was glad of the pain as it constantly reminded me of the loss. Your whole body aches physically with the loss; my breasts were painful for a few weeks afterwards, which was a consolation in a way, to be constantly reminded physically of that loss and grief.

It was unfortunate that I was under an unsympathetic consultant, and in the morning his registrar came to examine me . . . Flicking open my notes, he boomed, 'I see you had a pain in the tummy and started to bleed.' He removed the placenta with surprising gentleness, but rather crossly as there was no nurse with him. 'Never there when you want them,' he muttered and swept out of the cubicle leaving the curtains open . . . It was a mixed ward . . . but lying there with my legs apart, open to the gaze of strange men and women, I didn't feel anger – a sort of bemused objectiveness at my own passiveness, as if losing the baby I had lost my spirit. Here I was, articulate, middle class, intelligent, charming and a fighter by nature, magically transformed into Mrs Thing of Rochdale.

After the ERPC [evacuation of retained products of conception] at midday, I had a scan in the afternoon. Apparently my uterus was too large and there might be more placenta. The doctor doing the scan said it was a perfectly normal size for a seventeen- or eighteen-week fetus and my uterus was 'as clean as a whistle'. Meanwhile, back in the ward, I was unable to have any painkillers as nothing had been prescribed, and when the nurse rang 'my' doctor she was told I could buy some Panadol when I was discharged . . .

I had an outpatients' appointment a week later and saw a new doctor, a sweet, nervous houseman who told me I had an incompetent cervix and I could only be investigated after five miscarriages . . . I was told to have another scan and possibly ERPC as my uterus was still too large, but, fortunately, I discovered (via my GP) that the hospital letter stated I had fibroids* and a fourteen-week fetus removed. Obviously, my notes had been mixed up with someone else, so I never discovered why I had miscarried, nor the sex of the baby. My GP was useless, he didn't want to talk about it, and in a way I felt sorry for him as I knew what a lot of trouble he and his wife had been through with several miscarriages, but also felt sorry for myself because he had not been able to work through his own grief.†

Nothing had prepared me for the despair, the emptiness of grieving for an 'it'. The sheer murderous anger – I didn't know how to behave. The casual attitude of the hospital, the blankness of the GP and the absence of any practical help or information confused me. Was I meant to behave as if it had never happened? In a way I needed permission to grieve. If I had not had husband, friends and family, I shudder to think how I would have coped. I felt jealous of my husband who seemed to have more sympathetic support from his colleagues; most of my friends had never been pregnant, or were pregnant, and I felt as if I was bad luck, almost a failure – the spectre at the wedding feast. Because pregnancy and childbirth are now safe, there seems to be an almost neurotic compulsion by our society to stress only the happy positive side. The

*See page 64.

†An important point. See pages 194–7 on the emotional responses of medical staff to miscarriage.

fact that there is a sadder side is glossed over. The books on pregnancy I read at times made me furious. They seemed to be like estate agents' blurb. I found midwifery textbooks more comforting. At least there one could find out the cold hard facts, the truth, without all the rosy image of the 'happy, fulfilling etc. etc.' picture the books on pregnancy painted. I wanted to go to a clairvoyant to find out the sex of the child, but my husband being a Calvinistic Scot was shocked by the suggestion.

The grief and anger became less as time went on; we moved flats, went on holiday and I started a new job. All three events had been planned before I was pregnant.

I distrusted my body. Perhaps I could never have children, and I couldn't imagine my life without them . . . I had to get pregnant again, I had to be pregnant when the first baby would have been born in February, and as each period arrived I was thrown into a despairing depression.

Three months after the miscarriage, I became pregnant again.

Second (twin) pregnancy:

All through that pregnancy I felt pulled in opposite directions. In one direction, or as my pregnant self, I felt if I stopped concentrating on the pregnancy, I would miscarry. (Exactly in the way in which people with flying phobia think that if they stop concentrating on the pilot, the plane will crash.) The other direction, or non-pregnant me, couldn't believe I was pregnant, and I can well understand the lonely illogical world of the neurotic with an *idée fixe*. I knew I was pregnant, and later on it was obvious I was, but I didn't believe it. I felt a fraud collecting maternity benefit, free dental treatment etc. I bought nothing and any gifts for the new baby were stored carefully away, still in the wrappers so I could take them back to the shop after the unhappy event.

If anyone remarked on my pregnant state, in one way

it pleased me, in another, it threw me into confusion. In this non-pregnant state, tea, coffee, alcohol and cigarettes did not nauseate me, thus confirming my deepest suspicions that I wasn't pregnant any more.

My constant fear was that the hospital would take my babies away from me. I had enough insight to know it was impossible, unless I was very ill – or, my greatest fear, that I had gone mad. Knowing this was unlikely, yet fearing it, seemed to be like being pulled again in two directions; what I used to call my mad state and my un-mad state. I had a good disguise, few people realized how anxious and unhappy I was. Even with people I loved and trusted (except my husband and NCT* teacher) I couldn't drop my mask, because I felt if I did, I would disintegrate. There is only one photograph of me when pregnant, and coming across it by chance the other day, I was struck by how unlike me it was. There was a stillness in the face like old Victorian photos.

I had terrible nightmares. The two recurring ones I still remember vividly. Sometimes, I would be bleeding, and I would jerk awake, tense and alert, trying to summon up the courage to check if I was, unable to differentiate between dreaming and being awake. The other nightmare would be where I was holding twins, but gradually, they would become smaller and smaller, and more like dolls than babies; or they would disappear and I would be frantically searching for them, calling out for help. But the people were shadowy and didn't seem to understand what I was looking for. Sometimes, it was only one baby I was holding that would disappear, and in my dreams I would scramble through drawers and cupboards searching frantically.

Sleep was difficult – even in the early months I would wake early. I never rested or 'took things easy'. Eating was another difficulty, but at least I never had a weight problem in that pregnancy. I took laxatives regularly as I didn't dare strain. Every time I removed my pants I
* National Childbirth Trust.

expected to see blood, and in the end I stopped wearing any. I never felt the twins moving, and I don't know whether I refused to recognize the kicking or what. I couldn't bear thinking about my body from the neck down. The sight of pregnant women made me shudder. In my mind, there was no connection between pregnancy and babies, since prams, babies etc. had no adverse effect on me.*

My GP, I knew, was useless, but I didn't want to change him. Firstly, because when I went for my antenatals we chatted about other things. There were no pregnant women about, and I wasn't obliged to act 'pregnant'. Secondly, as his wife had had so much trouble in hospital with her miscarriages, he understood when I refused to go to any more antenatals there. He unhesitatingly wrote a letter to the consultant saying that I had been so upset after the last antenatal visit that he would look after my pregnancy until the thirty-second week . . .

When I was 33 weeks pregnant the waters ruptured early one morning. I went into a state of near panic. I was shaking and crying so much I could hardly dress . . . A sort of passiveness took over when I managed to stop shaking, and waiting for the ambulance, I made plans for the future. I couldn't face another pregnancy, I didn't have the courage. There were parallels with the last time, the suddenness, the way the cat shot out of the front door with his tail in the air and pirouetted about the empty street . . .

It all ended happily. I was amazed to find two live babies at the end. I had refused to even think of the possibility – they really were like two little strangers whom I was meeting for the first time without any preconception of what they would be like . . .

A few months later, we were out for a walk *en famille*, happy and contented, until we passed the hospital where

* The two themes of denying the reality of pregnancy and having especially vivid dreams are echoed by other women: see pages 171–2.

the first pregnancy had ended, and a sudden burst of grief and bitterness hit me. For a brief second, the twins meant nothing . . .

When the twins were seven months old, we went on holiday to Wales, and by now I had come to terms with my miscarriage. I still had moments of bitterness . . . usually when I heard of someone who had a miscarriage and had known what sex the baby was, but I accepted it as one of the sad facts of life. At three in the morning one of the twins woke to be fed, and after I had put him back into the cot, I fell instantly asleep. I began to dream I was talking to a middle-aged woman, telling her how much I wanted to know what the sex of the first baby was. Although it was a dream, parts of it were more real than being awake. The woman was about to write down on a pad 'male' or 'female' when a clear voice said 'No', very emphatically. We were sitting in a large blue room, and as she took my right hand, a thin, rather nondescript man came in and took my left hand. I was told to concentrate hard on the fetus, which I found I could do without much effort – it seemed to fill my mind. I must have been crying as the man was stroking my hand to comfort me. There was a feeling of tremendous force in the room and the sound of rushing wind encircling us. It was quite frightening, and I began to think that it was evil, but even as I thought that, a feeling of goodness came to me. Suddenly, the noise stopped. Everyone was laughing joyfully and there was bright light everywhere. We were no longer holding hands, and, looking at me, the woman said, 'Look behind you.' I was now two people, I could see myself, yet I was still myself (almost like a mirror, but it was closer than that, there was no break). I turned and saw a baby, about a year old, sitting in a baby chair. I knew who he was, and was struck by some family resemblances. As I ran to him, the voice said, 'His name is Thomas'. Cradling him in my arms, I felt complete peace and joy. Space and time had no meaning, there was no break with my life 'on earth' . . . As I rocked him gently, I knew I would never see him again, but it didn't matter. He was quite a fragile looking boy, about seventeen pounds in weight. As I woke up, I could hear myself whispering 'thank you, thank you' over and over again. Tears were streaming from my eyes, and the pillow was damp, but they were tears of joy, not grief.

I will never forget, and always be grateful for, that dream. Over and over, I coolly went through it, trying to find a logical explanation; wishful thinking, too vivid an imagination, and so on. The name Thomas, although a family name, had never been on our short list of names. But one thing I could not ignore was the benefit it gave me. It freed me. The bond of the past had been severed. Part of me had still been embroiled in my miscarriage and difficult pregnancy, and now it was firmly in the past.

2 An Overview of Normal Early Pregnancy

Although a certain amount is known about why miscarriages occur, there is still an enormous amount to find out. This lack of information is one reason why women having miscarriages who ask their doctors about the causes of miscarriages commonly get unsatisfactory answers. Doctors don't know all the answers – and we tend to regard them as being more omniscient than they really are, or than some of them see themselves. Many women in our questionnaire survey reported being surprised that so little is known about miscarriage. It's not hard to make the connection between the lack of knowledge and the incompleteness of the research on the topic:

> I felt angry because the medical profession seemed to view an early miscarriage as a pretty inconsequential event and were not bothered about trying to determine why I had had two miscarriages. I also felt angry that someone like myself, reasonably intelligent and informed, was so ignorant about something so important. I blamed myself and 'the system' which provides information and advice only after the most crucial part of pregnancy is past. (Jane Walker)

Jane Walker's point is that we all ought to be more aware of the reality of miscarriage and interested in finding out about it. For some doctors, miscarriages are 'inconsequential' in the sense that they are usually followed, sooner or later, by successful pregnancy, and the impetus to research their causes may be less than the drive to engage in other areas of research, such as the technology of 'test-tube' babies.

Another reason why we don't know more about miscarriage is because of the complexity of the large number of subtly interdependent factors which lead to a normal pregnancy and delivery. It is not therefore surprising that miscarriages occur fairly frequently, and that (as we shall see) in many cases what is miscarried is an abnormal fetus. In this sense it could even be argued that the word 'miscarriage' is inappropriate, because when an *abnormal* fetus fails to develop, this could be considered a positive event rather than a negative one. The doctor who attended Jane Walker, for example,

> made a valiant effort to console me with statistics about the large numbers of miscarriages that occur, saying also that it probably meant that the baby was abnormal. While I was in dire pain, I took some comfort from these thoughts . .

While rationally one may know a miscarriage could have been 'all for the best', emotionally there is still a necessity to grieve. Believing the fetus to have been abnormal doesn't always lessen the feeling of sadness: as another woman who had an early miscarriage observed:

> I know it is best to lose an imperfect baby – but the loss coincides with the ambivalent period you have at the start of pregnancy. Half feeling the pregnancy was a bad idea (even though planned) increases your sense of guilt when you do miscarry.

Nevertheless this positive feature of miscarriage – the loss of what would in some cases have been a deformed baby – is all too often forgotten. In fact, given the complexity of the reproductive process, perhaps one should be amazed that by far the majority of babies who are actually born do not have anything seriously wrong with them – in Britain in 1981 at least 97 per cent of babies did not have any serious abnormality. An alternative, more appropriate word for miscarriage might be 'disconception', but because of the common usage of the word 'miscarriage' we will continue to use it in this book.

We will try to explain what is known about miscarriage by briefly describing the normal anatomy and hormonal changes in the woman's body during the menstrual cycle and early pregnancy, and the normal formation and genetic makeup of the fertilized egg; we will then use this information to see where problems which lead to the fetus being lost early in pregnancy may occur, and how they may be treated. These problems include chromosomal and other abnormalities in the fetus, structural abnormalities in the reproductive system of the mother, hormonal problems, infections and other environmental causes.

With such a common event, you might wonder why all the processes are not yet clearly understood. One reason, as already suggested, is the complexity of the whole system, but other very real problems concern both the collection and the recollection of information. Finding out how many women miscarry, and when during pregnancy this happens, is difficult on many counts. Many women miscarry without realizing that they have been pregnant at all. Some women, even if they are aware that they have miscarried, see no reason to tell anyone, either because there are no associated problems, or because they did not want to be pregnant in the first place, and are therefore simply relieved. Because it is such a common and 'normal' phenomenon, some women do not even go to their GPs when it happens, or those that do, do not necessarily go into hospital (where many of the studies on the incidence of miscarriage are done). In our questionnaire survey of miscarriage, some guide to these 'selection' processes is that in 6 per cent of the miscarriages no doctor was contacted, and in 22 per cent the mother did not go into hospital. There may therefore be quite a large gap between the information wanted by those trying to do research into the incidence and causes of miscarriage, and the need to give such information as perceived by those who actually miscarry. For all these reasons, accurate information about how many women have miscarried in any population is hard to come by.

Recollection of information is also a problem because of the selective way our memories tend to work. If you have children, you know, for example, that if one of them has a headache, a previous bump will immediately be remembered to explain it, although children bump their heads all the time without getting headaches. You are therefore much more likely to remember details of every tablet taken, and every cough or sneeze, to try to provide a rational explanation as to why such a 'mishap' as miscarriage should have happened. This is the 'Why me?' question, and it is not confined to miscarriage: people have a need to understand why unpleasant events, such as illness and accidents, happen to them. It is extremely difficult to establish whether or not there are causal connections between the event in question and the recollected incident. What else happened that is not remembered? Does it make sense as an explanation to suppose, for example, that falling downstairs could lead to miscarriage, or that stress in pregnancy is a cause of Down's syndrome (mongolism) – an explanation put forward in the 1950s but subsequently discredited by the arrival of the 'genetic' explanation?

The women who filled in our questionnaires sometimes had views about what had caused their own miscarriages, and we describe these later (pages 114–16). As a prelude to our discussion of what is known about the causes of miscarriage, we give in this chapter an overview of normal early pregnancy. Although women have a good idea of how their bodies work, a brief résumé of normal reproduction is a helpful background to looking at the problems that can occur.

The physiology of normal early pregnancy

1. Diagram of women's reproductive organs (figures 2.1 and 2.2)
When talking about women's genitalia and reproductive organs, one is referring to the ovaries, the uterus (body of the womb), the cervix (neck of the womb), the fallopian tubes, the vagina, the labia and the clitoris. The ovaries are organs which both release the eggs and act as glands producing hormones (see below). The eggs are actually produced in the ovary of the female fetus during the early weeks of development, and a woman is born with all the eggs she will have – approximately 400,000 – more than enough to last many reproductive lifetimes.

2. Shedding of the egg
When a girl reaches about twelve or thirteen and starts having periods, an egg is normally released from her ovary each month, and this is directed into the mouth of the fallopian tubes by movements of the fimbriae (finger-like tentacles) which are at the opening of the fallopian tubes. This process continues until the menopause. If a woman makes love around the middle of the month when the egg is released, and is not using contraception, sperm will be swimming their way up the fallopian tubes to meet the egg as it makes its way down.

In many cases, for one reason or another, even if there is sperm around, the egg may not join with it and any actual meeting of these two may not be until twenty-four hours or more after intercourse. If the two meet and join this is called fertilization, and it is at this point that many people consider conception has taken place and the woman becomes pregnant. Over the next few days the fertilized egg descends into the womb. The fertilized egg then implants itself into the wall of the uterus, which has become specially prepared to receive it by the hormones, including progesterone and oestrogen, which have been released into the body (see below). The placenta develops in the part of the wall of the

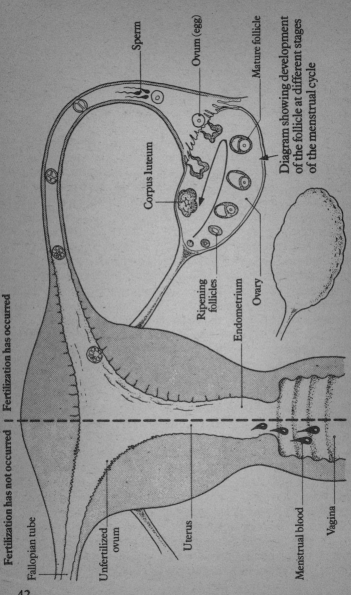

Fertilization has not occurred | Fertilization has occurred

Fallopian tube

Unfertilized ovum

Uterus

Menstrual blood

Vagina

Sperm

Ovum (egg)

Mature follicle

Diagram showing development
of the follicle at different stages
of the menstrual cycle

Corpus luteum

Ripening
follicles

Endometrium

Ovary

Figure 2.1 The uterus, fallopian tubes and ovaries (cross section) Figure 2.2 The ovary (from the outside)

womb where this implantation occurs and continues to develop throughout pregnancy.

The further development of the fetus over the first 24 weeks is outlined in the diagrams below (figures 2.3–2.7).

Normal hormone changes in the menstrual cycle

The most important hormones involved in the control of the menstrual cycle and menstruation are made either in the pituitary gland of the brain (luteinizing hormone, LH; follicle stimulating hormone, FSH; prolactin) or in the ovary (oestrogen, oestradiol and progesterone). Although these two organs are quite widely separated in the body, one of the fascinating things is that they send chemical signals to one another at critical times in the menstrual cycle to enable the egg to grow and be released from the ovary at ovulation in a predictable way. If the signals fail, then ovulation may never take place, the egg is not released, and hence pregnancy cannot occur.

The rises and falls of the different hormones during the menstrual cycle are confusing, and it is difficult to know where in the cycle to begin the story. If one looks at the hormone changes just before a period starts, then the pituitary gland is putting out hormone signals and producing increasing amounts of FSH to stimulate the growth of several cells called follicles in the ovary. During menstruation FSH levels continue to increase but, in general, one follicle only will grow more rapidly than the others and house the developing egg. We do not understand what determines the selection of this follicle. As it grows, it makes increasing amounts of oestrogen hormone (oestradiol) and when the level of this hormone reaches a certain critical point it signals the pituitary gland to pour out a surge of pituitary into the bloodstream. If we consider that a 'normal' menstrual cycle lasts 28 days (in some women it is shorter, and in some longer), then the oestrogen levels will have been rising steadily until about day 12, and the hormones will surge out

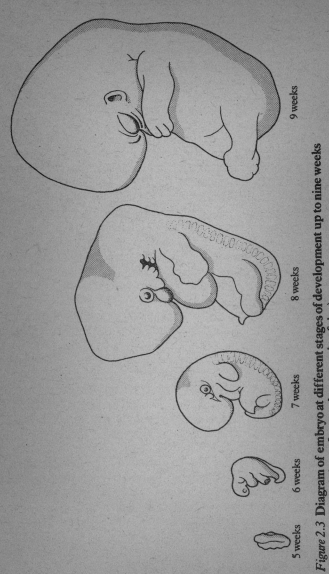

5 weeks   6 weeks   7 weeks   8 weeks   9 weeks

Figure 2.3 Diagram of embryo at different stages of development up to nine weeks (actual size at five weeks = a grain of rice)

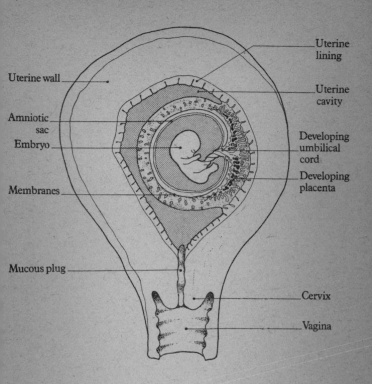

Figure 2.4 **Eight weeks pregnant: the baby is just one inch long**

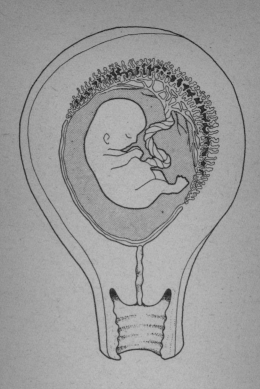

Figure 2.5 **Twelve weeks pregnant: the baby is now just over two inches long**

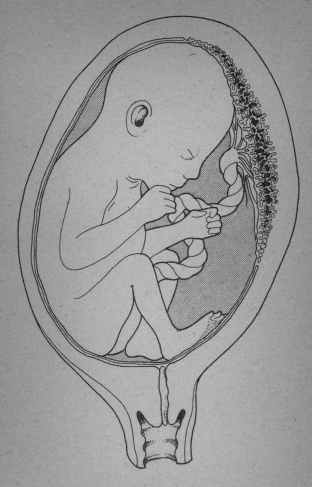

Figure 2.6 **Twenty weeks pregnant: the baby is now about ten inches long**

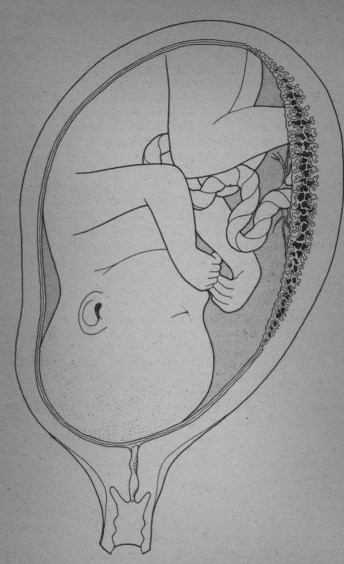

Figure 2.7 **Twenty-four weeks pregnant: the baby is now about thirteen inches long**

of the pituitary on the following day and then decline again. About 30 to 36 hours after the surge of pituitary hormones (day 14 of the cycle), the egg is shed from the follicle in the ovary and ovulation has taken place. The ruptured follicle, having released the ovum, then develops into the corpus luteum or yellow body, so-called because it looks yellow, which produces increasing amounts of the two hormones (oestradiol and progesterone). Levels of these two hormones rise together in the blood-stream until they reach a peak between days 18 and 22 of a 28-day cycle. If the egg is not fertilized, i.e., if pregnancy has not occurred, then the corpus luteum degenerates, its hormones fall away and a period occurs a few days later.

If you are muddled by all the hormones (it's difficult not to be!), it might help to look at the diagram on page 50.

Hormone changes in early pregnancy

Events at the beginning of pregnancy are different for the fetus and for the mother. For the fetus, pregnancy starts at the moment of fertilization, but no signals of pregnancy are sent to the mother until several days later, when the fertilized egg has reached the inside of the womb and implants on its wall. At this time, even though the fertilized egg is not much more than the size of a pinhead, it sends out a message to the mother and to her ovary to stop her menstrual cycle. Unlike the females of some other animal species (e.g., rabbits), women do not go on producing eggs during pregnancy. The corpus luteum in the ovary, instead of 'disappearing' as it usually does at the end of the menstrual cycle, remains functioning until after delivery of the baby, although it is not very active after the first 6–9 weeks of pregnancy. If there are many aspects of miscarriage that are not yet understood, many of the processes of normal pregnancy are still something of a mystery. One of these mysteries is 'what keeps the corpus luteum alive in pregnancy?' A popular theory is that the factor responsible is a hormone called

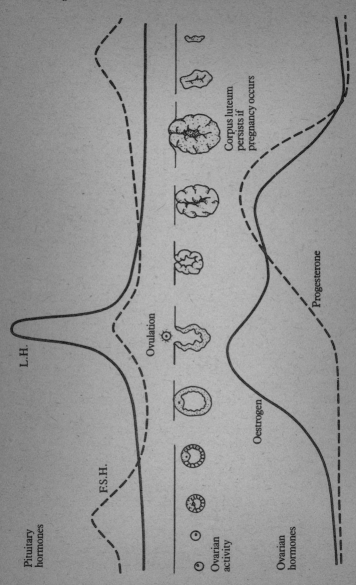

Pituitary hormones

L.H.

F.S.H.

Ovulation

Corpus luteum persists if pregnancy occurs

Ovarian activity

Oestrogen

Progesterone

Ovarian hormones

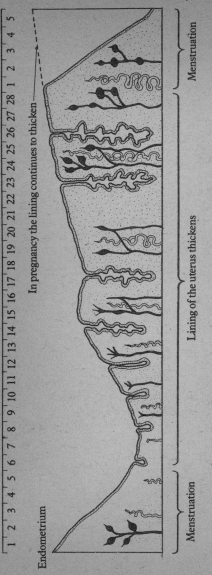

Days

In pregnancy the lining continues to thicken

Menstruation

Lining of the uterus thickens

Menstruation

Endometrium

Figure 2.8 **Changes in the body and in hormones during the menstrual cycle**

human chorionic gonadotrophin (HCG), probably made inside the womb by the developing placenta immediately after implantation of the fertilized egg. New and very sensitive tests to detect HCG in the urine are now available. These are used as a way of diagnosing pregnancy very early – about a week before a period is even missed. We have mentioned this hormone, HCG, as it is sometimes thought to be deficient and is given as a treatment to prevent miscarriage (see pages 146–77).

Although there are doubts about what controls the corpus luteum, there is no doubt that its function is absolutely vital for the maintenance of early pregnancy. If a woman's ovaries or the corpus luteum are removed in early pregnancy then miscarriage will occur. The most reliable estimate is that the corpus luteum is vital until 6–7 weeks after the first day of the last period. During the early weeks of pregnancy it is the hormone progesterone produced in increasing amounts by the corpus luteum which seems to be essential for maintaining the pregnancy.

Chromosomes in normal pregnancy

An important component in the story of normal early pregnancy concerns the messenger materials contained within the fertilized egg, which dictate how the fetus develops the way that it does.

These messenger materials, called chromosomes, are present in the nucleus of every cell in the body including the egg and sperm cells. Each chromosome is a package of thousands of genes, chemical units that control individual cellular functions. The chromosomes transmit basic genetic characteristics from parents to child, for example colour of eyes, height, colour of hair, shape of the nose, etc. They also dictate the sex of the baby.

Every normal person has 46 chromosomes arranged in 23 pairs (one of each pair is inherited from each parent) inside the nucleus of every cell. There are two exceptions – the egg

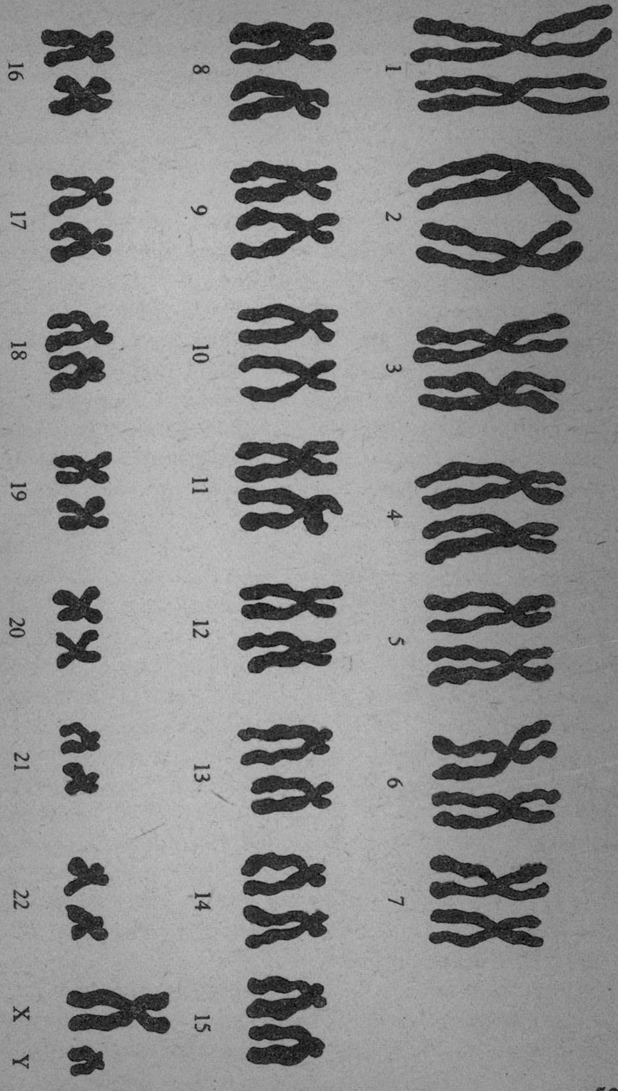

Figure 2.9 Normal pairs of chromosomes

cell and the sperm cell, which each have 23 chromosomes instead of 46.

Looking at them under a microscope, each of the 23 pairs of chromosomes is slightly different from the other pairs. To make things easier, each pair has been given a number by geneticists. The largest pair is no. 1, the smallest pair no. 22, and there are another two chromosomes called X and Y which determine the sex of the baby. XX is a female and XY is a male.

During the normal growth and division of body cells (a process going on all the time in most cells of your body), the chromosomes duplicate and make an exact copy of themselves. This process, called mitosis, means that every new cell has the same number of chromosomes as every old one.

The cells in the ovary and testes undergo a different kind of division called meiosis. This type of division reduces the chromosomes from 46 to 23, so that egg and sperm cells each have only one of each type of chromosome. At conception a 23 chromosome egg and a 23 chromosome sperm meet and join together, and the fertilized egg from which a baby develops then has 46 chromosomes – one set from the mother and one from the father. It is easy to imagine how many things might go wrong with all this dividing and joining up again.

The experience of early pregnancy

Before we move on to look at what can go wrong in these early pregnancy processes to bring about miscarriage, it might be helpful to say a little bit about women's experiences of early pregnancy. The physiological drama is being unfolded inside the body, but how is this translated into the mother's thoughts and feelings?

On a physical level, the first sign of pregnancy is most often a missed period. However, other signs are not infrequent: in table 2.1 we give the first sign of pregnancy noticed by a group of women having their first babies in London in the mid-1970s.

Table 2.1 **First pregnancy symptoms**

	%
Missed period	62
Nausea and/or vomiting	12
Sore breasts	9
Light period	5
'Felt pregnant'	3
Frequent urination	2
Other	6

Source: Oakley, 1981

Nausea or vomiting, which come second in this list, are experienced often in the first three months by around half of all pregnant women according to a number of studies. There is some suggestion that if you have pronounced nausea and vomiting, you are more likely to have a girl than a boy. (This is one among a number of 'old wives' tales' shown by scientific medicine to have some truth to it – the suggested explanation being that the level of hormones contributing to pregnancy nausea is higher with female than male fetuses.)

Women's emotional responses to early pregnancy reflect both the physical symptoms and the social and personal significance of pregnancy. For example, if you are feeling very tired or nauseated, then however much you wanted to be pregnant, there is bound to be an element of 'my God, what have I let myself in for?' Pregnancy and motherhood are experiences which profoundly alter not only women's bodies but the whole pattern of their lives, so what has to be adjusted to in pregnancy is an anticipated life-change of a major kind. Table 2.2 is taken from the same study as the earlier one and shows reactions to confirmation of pregnancy among this group of women (most of whom had wanted to be pregnant).

A very similar pattern of reactions was found in an American study – so there is nothing peculiar about women in London!

Table 2.2 **First reactions to pregnancy**

	%
Pleased	52
Mixed feelings	38
Upset	11

Source: Oakley, 1981

Another seemingly normal feature of early pregnancy is the tendency to worry about the pregnancy, the fetus and oneself. About two-fifths of women in the London study said they worried about having a deformed baby. Much the same proportion worried about the change in life style that a successful pregnancy would mean. Such anxieties are stronger early in pregnancy and most women in both these studies worried about the possibility of miscarriage. Along with the higher anxiety tends to go more self-preoccupation, the capacity to become easily upset and a greater need for emotional support from family and friends. It seems likely that these mental and emotional reactions to early pregnancy are due to many factors, including each woman's personal history and the social context in which she is currently living, and the hormonal changes within her body. Whether or not the pregnancy was planned to happen at that time doesn't seem to be a major factor affecting the pattern of reactions – an unplanned pregnancy can be a cause of joy just as a planned pregnancy may bring about an unexpected feeling of ambivalence. We can see the same paradox with respect to miscarriages, for the loss of an initially unplanned baby may be just as devastating as the loss of one whose conception was planned. Indeed, it may even be more so, for you have first to adjust to the shock of an unexpected pregnancy and then to the shock of its unexpected premature end. Of course early loss of a planned baby may also pass with little trauma.

One of the points we are making here is that normal early pregnancy is not necessarily an unproblematic experience for the mother, either physically or emotionally. It is within this context that we look in the next chapter at some of the many things that may go wrong to cause miscarriage.

3 What Goes Wrong?

In perhaps about half of all miscarriages, it is possible to identify some factor or factors which must have contributed to the likelihood of miscarriage. This leaves a large proportion, of course, entirely unexplained – as yet. In this chapter we concentrate upon what *is* known about factors increasing a woman's chances of miscarriage.

One way to approach this is to divide up the factors into those arising in the fetus and those arising in the mother. There are also factors which appear to influence both fetus and mother – we have listed these in table 3.1. Of course, the father also has a role, but most of his contribution is included in the category of 'fetus'.

Table 3.1 **Factors which may affect miscarriage**

Fetus	*Mother*
Chromosomal	Anatomical
Non-chromosomal	Fibroids
	Dieseases (e.g., diabetes)
	Hormonal

Both/Other	
Mother's age	Occupation
Father's age	Work in pregnancy
Contraception	Stress
Previously induced abortion and miscarriage	Toxic chemicals
	Irradiation
Sexual intercourse and vaginal examination	Ultrasound
	Drugs
Alcohol	Immune mechanisms
Smoking	Infections
Diet	Accidents

The categories shown in table 3.1 are somewhat arbitrary, and not all the causes of miscarriage fall neatly into these boxes. In some cases there may be more than one factor responsible for the miscarriage.

Abnormalities in the fetus

It is well known that many miscarriages are due to abnormalities in the development of the fetus. In some way, the mother's body appears to recognize that a fetus is not developing and functioning normally, and some mechanism orders it to be expelled. People who have suffered miscarriages therefore often ask whether the fetus would have been abnormal if it had gone on to be born at term. Because of the considerable technical difficulties of studying miscarried fetuses, it is not often possible to give a definite answer in an individual case. Several studies have, however, shown that up to 50 per cent of miscarried fetuses have some sort of abnormality. This must be a minimum estimate, as many of the more subtle abnormalities, particularly those at a biochemical level, and those which cause later onset of developmental problems in babies, would not be detectable in a miscarried fetus.

Chromosomal factors

Most types of common abnormalities – spina bifida, heart disorders, and so on – are seen more commonly in fetuses than in liveborn children. The best-studied situation, however, is that of chromosome abnormalities, because chromosome tests can be done on small fragments of tissue, even when a whole fetus is not avilable to be looked at. There are many different kinds of chromosome abnormalities, mostly causing such severe developmental abnormalities that the affected pregnancies always miscarry. However, the less severe abnormalities such as Down's syndrome, Turner's syndrome (a sex chromosome abnormality), and several others seen in liveborn children, also generally appear more frequently in miscarriages. For example, 75 per cent of Down's syndrome pregnancies miscarry, as do about 95 per cent of pregnancies missing a sex chromosome, of the sort which give rise to Turner's syndrome in liveborn children. It is not known why some pregnancies miscarry, while others with an apparently identical chromosome makeup go through to term.

In general, most studies have found that chromosome abnormalities are frequent in miscarried fetuses, and that they are more frequent in the pregnancies which miscarry earlier than in those which miscarry later. It is not very easy to identify and study pregnancies which miscarry before about six or seven weeks, but at this stage, it appears that about 60 per cent of all pregnancies that do miscarry have chromosome abnormalities. Assuming that this trend continues backwards into even earlier stages of pregnancy, people have calculated that 10 per cent or more of all human conceptions may have chromosome abnormalities. Most of these, as already mentioned, would be lost so early on that the woman would hardly be aware that she is pregnant.

These chromosome abnormalities are almost all one-off accidents that occur during the formation of individual egg and sperm cells. They do not therefore carry any serious risk of recurring in future pregnancies of that couple. Occasionally, the situation does crop up where one or other parent actually carries a 'balanced chromosome abnormality', which does lead to that person forming a regular, and fairly high, proportion of chromosomally abnormal eggs or sperm. Such a person may have a higher than average risk of having a chromosomally abnormal child, and would certainly have a higher than average risk of producing pregnancies sufficiently severely affected to miscarry early on. Chromosomal causes are responsible for the repeated miscarriages of about 5 per cent of couples. Any couple who has had more than two or three miscarriages should therefore have a chromosome test as part of the investigation of this problem (see page 177).

Exposure to certain drugs and chemicals, and irradiation,

have sometimes been said to increase the risk of genetic and chromosome abnormalities. But in practice it is not understood how most chromosome abnormalities arise. We do know that many chromosome abnormalities, in liveborn and in miscarried pregnancies, become more common with advancing age, but even there we do not know why this happens.

The type of chromosome abnormality which increases with a mother's age is called a Trisomy, where one extra chromosome is present in each cell. Other chromosome abnormalities can also be categorized, but we will not go into the technicalities of what they mean, merely giving the names of the groups in case they are mentioned when your doctor talks to you about miscarriage.

Table 3.2 **The incidence of different types of chromosome abnormalities in miscarriages with chromosome abnormalities**

	%
Trisomy	50.1
Sex Chromosome Monosomy	19.9
Triploidy	15.0
Tetraploidy	5.0
Others	10.0
Total	100.0

Table 3.3 **The main chromosome abnormalities**

Trisomy	1 extra chromosome per cell (47)
Monosomy	1 chromosome too few per cell (45)
Triploidy	a complete extra set of chromosomes per cell (69)
Tetraploidy	twice the normal number of chromosomes (92)

Non-chromosomal factors

As already mentioned, the chromosomes and genes can be quite normal but there can be something else wrong with the anatomical structure of the developing fetus. Perhaps one of the best-known examples of this is spina bifida, in which the spinal cord of the baby does not develop properly. This is thought to be due to abnormal development of a group of cells in the fetus called the neural crest, from which the brain and spinal cord develop in the fifth and sixth week of pregnancy. Although many theories have been, and are still being put forward to explain spina bifida, the actual cause remains a mystery; we do, however, know that there is an increased chance of it occurring in a subsequent pregnancy given that it has happened once. Recent work suggests that taking vitamin and folic acid supplements before the next pregnancy may help to prevent a recurrence. For an individual woman the risk of recurrence is not enormous: it is thought that half of all fetuses which develop spina bifida end up by spontaneously miscarrying. Reported rates of spina bifida in live births are about 1.7 for every one thousand births. Other examples of anatomical abnormalities are anencephaly, when the baby develops without a brain, and exomphalos, in which it develops without a wall to its abdomen.

Maternal problems

Abnormalities of anatomy

We have described the normal anatomy of a woman, and of course it is sometimes possible for anatomical development not to be quite normal, thus making miscarriage more likely. Few good studies have been done to assess how often malformations of the womb cause problems, as these malformations will usually go undetected, especially as the baby develops normally and is born normally in most cases. Malformations of the womb can happen during a woman's own development as a fetus, following childbirth, or because of an operation. If one first looks at development of the uterus, it is clear that numerous variations are possible. When the womb forms it does so from the fusion of two primitive tubes. These can fail to fuse, or fuse abnormally. A few of the most common abnormalities are shown in the diagram below (figure 3.1) and even these are not very common. (For cervical incompetence, see page 149.)

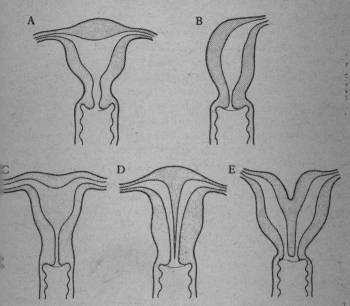

Figure 3.1 Normal uterus (A) and various uterine
           abnormalities (B-E)

Estimates as to how often such abnormalities occur vary from one in 1000 to two in 100 women. Some of the variations will not cause problems, but in others the abnormal womb will be unable to enlarge rapidly enough to accommodate the growing fetus. Because of the abnormal anatomy, the placenta may also implant on a part of the womb which has

Miscarriage

a poor blood supply. The frequency of miscarriage in the first three months does not appear to be increased by these abnormalities, but the frequency of miscarriage in the second three months of pregnancy does: as many as 25–50 per cent of pregnancies in women with double uteruses are lost in the middle three months. If a woman is miscarrying at this stage of pregnancy, it is worth obtaining a medical examination to exclude anatomical abnormality as a contributory cause. In some cases surgical correction is possible.

Fibroids

Fibroids are benign tumours of the womb. They are the commonest benign tumours (they are *not* cancers) in the human body and it is estimated that 20 per cent of all women have one or more present in the womb at some time. They usually cause no problems, but do occasionally cause heavy periods, especially if the fibroids occur in women in their late thirties and around the time of the menopause. Sometimes they are found after a woman has had a miscarriage or repeated miscarriages – but whether they have any part to play in this is unknown. As with malformations of the uterus, it is not known how many women with fibroids have a normal pregnancy, since the woman is only investigated if there is an obvious problem such as miscarriage. It is thought that fibroids occurring right inside the womb, called submucous fibroids, are more likely to cause miscarriages. There is little evidence that their removal improves your chances of having a baby following a miscarriage, but, if you are older, have a history of recurrent miscarriages, and no other cause for them is found, then removal of the fibroids is often recommended. Some women do then go on to have normal babies, but whether this is cause and effect is by no means certain.

Diseases

Certain illnesses, such as diabetes, kidney disease, high blood pressure and thyroid problems, may lead to complications in pregnancy. There is little evidence as to whether such diseases are associated with an increased risk of miscarriage, although if a woman has one of these illnesses, her pregnancy will be watched especially carefully.

Hormonal problems

Women's hormones are blamed for many so-called 'women's problems'. In the nineteenth century the idea was popularized that women are inherently unstable because they are constantly at the mercy of their menstrual cycles. This rather limited and insulting view of women was promoted especially by the medical profession of the time, and was used as an argument against educating women or 'permitting' them to engage in professional work. The argument is not quite dead yet, though in the twentieth century we have refined it somewhat, and now talk specifically about such things as 'premenstrual tension' and 'postnatal depression'. The ebb and flow of hormones with the menstrual cycle does seem to suggest some kind of instant explanation of women's behaviour, particularly of *negative* behaviour – i.e., behaviour which is antisocial and otherwise hazardous. (Female hormones are less often credited with *positive* achievement – women aren't said to get to the top with the aid of their hormones – but there isn't any reason to suppose this couldn't be true!)

Not surprisingly, hormonal problems are also thought to be one of the causes of miscarriage. As we have already shown in chapter 2, progesterone and HCG are important hormones involved in the maintenance of the pregnancy. This has led people to think that lack of one of these hormones might be a cause of miscarriage, and that if this is true, the way to treat it might be by giving the appropriate hormone to compensate for the body's own deficient production. The problem with this approach is that we really do not know very much about the role hormonal factors play in miscarriage. The necessary knowledge would demand studying the hormonal profiles of large numbers of women from (or before) conception onwards, and comparing the profiles of those who keep their pregnancies with the profiles of those who lose them. This is obviously a complicated exercise. In its place the approach used has been to give some kind of hormonal treatment to women at risk of miscarriage (women who have already miscarried once or more) and see if it has any effect in reducing the repeat miscarriage rate. Because this comes under the heading of 'treatment' we look at the evidence for and against it in chapter 7.

Other factors

Mother's age

There is little doubt that the risk of a spontaneous miscarriage increases with age and that this increase is most marked after thirty. Interestingly, this increased risk applies to both chromosomally abnormal and chromosomally normal fetuses. Thus, all the trisomy abnormalities which we mentioned in the section dealing with genetic problems are related to maternal age, with an increased incidence in older women. So the older you are, the more likely you are to have a miscarriage, and, if you do miscarry, it's more likely that the fetus will be abnormal, but you're also more likely to miscarry a normal fetus than younger women. There are, however, a few very rare chromosomal abnormalities which may occur more frequently at a young age.

Father's age

It does seem that the 'blame' or the cause for miscarriage is most often looked for in the mother. Evidence regarding paternal roles in miscarriage is scanty, and this is the case with the possible link between the risk of miscarriage and paternal age. One study shows that when the father of the offspring is elderly there is an association with an increased incidence of miscarriage which is *stronger* than the association with increased maternal age. Other studies do not, however, confirm this. One theory for the possible paternal effect is that intercourse becomes less frequent with increasing age; the sperm are therefore older, and older sperm are more likely to have an abnormality and therefore produce an increased risk of miscarriage. At the moment, the consensus is that the father's age really has little effect, but perhaps this evidence will change with further investigation.

Contraception

When considering the relation between contraception and miscarriage one needs to know the answers to certain questions.

(a) Does the method of contraception used, and then stopped, before getting pregnant increase the likely risk of miscarriage?

(b) Does the method of contraception increase the risk of miscarriage if the method fails and one gets pregnant while using it?

THE PILL

The pill is still the method of contraception most widely used by young people. There seems to be no increased risk of having a miscarriage if you have been using the pill and stopped it prior to getting pregnant; in fact, one study showed that there is a *decreased* incidence of miscarriage. Another study showed that if one did miscarry after getting pregnant having stopped taking the pill, the fetus was more likely to have chromosomal abnormalities. These two findings may not, in fact, be contradictory if one supposes that the 'pill effect' is to reduce miscarriage among chromosomally normal fetuses, but leave unaffected the chances of losing a chromosomally abnormal fetus.

If one gets pregnant while using the pill there may be a very slight increased risk of miscarriage, but once again not all studies show this. We found in our questionnaire survey that some women did feel the pill could have been partly responsible for their miscarriages (see page 114) – they could be right, but, as we have said, there is really no firm statistical proof one way or the other.

BARRIER METHODS

The sheath and/or spermicide are widely used – they are the most popular in certain age groups and social classes. The diaphragm is also used by a fair number of British women trying to avoid pregnancy. Neither the sheath nor the diaphragm appear to have any effect on miscarriage rates. Although spermicides have been known for thousands of years (the ancient Egyptians used crocodile dung!), their relationship with miscarriage has not been evaluated. Most of the studies that have been done looking at modern chemical spermicide use before and at the time of conception showed no association with miscarriage, although recently an American study suggested that there might be a possible association. But criticisms can be levelled at the way these data were collected and the way in which spermicidal use was statistically related to miscarriage, so once again we are left with incomplete evidence. Suffice to say that if there is any increased risk of miscarriage associated with use of spermicides, it must be very small indeed.

IUCD/COIL

Some 5–10 per cent of women use the IUCD (intrauterine contraceptive device) or coil as a form of contraception. It works by preventing the ovum from becoming implanted but does not prevent fertilization. There is nothing to show that if you use a coil and have it removed before getting pregnant you are more likely subsequently to miscarry. However, the IUCD is not a perfect contraceptive and a small number of women do get pregnant while using it. If a pregnancy occurs there is an increased risk of miscarriage whatever type of IUCD is used, and whether the IUCD is left in or removed: but the risk of miscarriage is three times greater if it is left in, and this risk may be as great as 50 per cent. One might think this high risk of miscarriage does not matter if the mother does not want the pregnancy. After all, if there are no complications it could be seen as a good way to terminate the pregnancy. Unfortunately, there is a serious risk of infection if the IUCD is left in place. Therefore, the advice is – whether one wants the pregnancy or not – to have the coil removed as soon as the pregnancy is diagnosed. If you want to be pregnant, the chances are that you will carry on and have a normal pregnancy and normal delivery after the coil is out (although there is an increased risk of miscarriage and premature labour throughout pregnancy). If you don't want the pregnancy, then a termination needs to be arranged at the same time as, or subsequent to, coil removal. There is no evidence that a coil causes increased abnormalities in the fetus.

Previous induced abortion and miscarriage

When women get pregnant by mistake and want a termination of pregnancy, two of the questions they often want answered are, 'Will it affect my future fertility?' and, 'Will it increase the chance of my having a miscarriage with my next pregnancy?' It is important to know the answer to both questions to be able to give this information to women seeking an abortion. So what are the facts? Numerous studies have tried to unravel the many factors that could possibly alter a woman's chances of successful pregnancy following a termination. These factors include the stage in the pregnancy when the termination was done, and the method used (see below). Studies have also tried to look at the effect on subsequent pregnancies of a D & C done for reasons other than terminating pregnancy (for instance to investigate heavy periods or because of infertility). To summarize all this research we can say that the evidence is that a single induced abortion or a previous D & C for other reasons is unlikely to raise the risk of subsequent miscarriage in the first three months of pregnancy. We don't have enough evidence to make a definite statement on the effect on future pregnancies of having *many* induced abortions. It is also difficult to evaluate whether induced abortion raises the risk of miscarriage in the middle three months of pregnancy, but it does seem as though there may be a slightly increased risk – especially in those women who have *only* had an induced abortion before, and no previous full-term pregnancies as well. According to the research done, the risk was greatest for those women who had their abortions prior to 1973, and it is thought that the methods then used to induce an abortion by instrumentally dilating the cervix were the cause of this extra risk. Nowadays, most early terminations are done by suction or using prostaglandin drugs put into the cervix rather than by dilation and curettage, and these newer methods are much less likely to damage the cervix.

It is important to place this evidence of the possible hazards of induced abortion in perspective. Many women worry about the future consequences of having an abortion, and a woman who *does* have a miscarriage may well fasten on to her previous abortion and blame herself for 'causing' her miscarriage. But having had an abortion is really most unlikely to be the main cause of an individual woman's miscarriage. One study calculated that fewer than 4 per cent of spontaneous abortions could be attributed to previous induced abortion, so that on those figures one can be very reassuring.

Sexual intercourse and vaginal examinations

Many people wonder whether sexual intercourse can be a cause of miscarriage. Women are especially likely to worry about this if they have had a miscarriage, afterwards sought for a reason, and remembered that they had intercourse in the few days before it happened.

Old obstetric textbooks were full of reasons as to why women should not have intercourse during pregnancy. Risk of infection, premature labour and miscarriage have all been claimed to occur more often if women are sexually active while pregnant. Some of these claims clearly have a great deal more to do with sexual mores and attitudes towards women than with the results of careful scientific studies. Although women experiencing repeated miscarriage are still widely advised to abstain from intercourse during the first three months of pregnancy, there is no scientific evidence that intercourse causes miscarriage. None of the many theories as to how intercourse might cause miscarriage really stands up to examination. One theory, for example, is that orgasm and the associated uterine contractions might play some part. If this is so, then it is difficult to know how to advise the 5–10 per cent of women who are said to have orgasms in their dreams!

Anxieties about medical vaginal examinations as a cause of miscarriage are also very common. When you think you are pregnant and go to your doctor early in pregnancy, the routine examination does usually include a vaginal examination. The doctor looks at your cervix using a speculum and then with one hand on your tummy and the other feeling you internally will judge how big your uterus is, and whether it is the 'right size for dates' (i.e., that the uterus has grown to the size it should have done by the date of your last period). After you are twelve weeks pregnant, the top of the womb can just be felt by putting a hand on your tummy and assessing the growth of the baby.

A woman who starts to bleed soon after an internal examination is very likely to associate the two. There is no good evidence that an internal examination actually causes a miscarriage: any association between the examination and threatened miscarriage is probably chance. However, we do know that later on in pregnancy, feeling and stimulating the cervix can result in the release of hormones which are involved in the onset of labour. Therefore, some obstetricians do not do an internal examination early in pregnancy if there has been a previous miscarriage or a history of several miscarriages. It makes sense to avoid any unnecessary internal examinations – not least because most women find them very uncomfortable.

Alcohol

As early as 1781 a Dublin midwifery professor stated that 'the abuse of strong liquor' could lead to uterine haemorrhage and miscarriage. Advice about drinking in pregnancy has recently changed. It used to be considered all right to have an occasional drink – but now the message is

71

Miscarriage

that even quite small amounts of alcohol taken by the mother may have a harmful effect on the fetus. Two recent studies have looked at miscarriage and alcohol consumption. In one of these there was only an increase in the number of miscarriages in the second three months when alcohol was consumed throughout the pregnancy. In the other study, there were more miscarriages at all times with alcohol consumption, even if the amount of drinking was very small (as little as one glass of wine twice a week), but the effect was greater with heavier drinking. We know almost nothing about the effect on the risk of miscarriage of 'binge' drinking, different types of alcohol, whether or not the alcohol is taken with food, or the combined action of smoking and alcohol. Again, we feel this new emphasis on the harmful effects of alcohol must be put into perspective. Most mothers who have drunk alcohol in 'social' quantities during pregnancy have normal babies, and do not have a miscarriage. However, as we have said, there does seem to be an association between miscarriage and alcohol; it is thought that the alcohol can act as a poison to the highly sensitive developing fetus. Drinking prior to getting pregnant does not appear to be a risk factor in miscarriage. As with many other factors, the contribution of male drinking to miscarriage has not really been looked at, so we do not know how dangerous it is (from the fetus's point of view) for fathers-to drink.

Smoking

More and more associations are being discovered between smoking and disease. Yet in a recent government survey more than half the people questioned still did not believe that smoking damages health. In 1982, 11 per cent of secondary schoolchildren in Britain reported that they smoked regularly.

Smoking during pregnancy is associated with a reduction in the size of babies, which are then more at risk from a whole variety of factors. The babies of mothers who smoke during pregnancy are slightly more likely to die around the time of birth. Smoking does also appear to be associated with an increased likelihood of miscarriage, especially between the fourth and seventh month. Women who miscarry are almost twice as likely as those who don't miscarry to be smokers. However, we do not really know whether the smoking causes the miscarriage or whether both the tendency to smoke and the tendency to miscarry are related to some other factor or factors. The chances of a baby being less healthy are increased when the number of cigarettes smoked is large, so this suggests that smoking is not a good thing and that, if you can't give up completely, it is definitely worth cutting down the number of cigarettes you smoke. Although little research has been done on the reproductive effects of smoking in men, there are suggestions that it may impair fertility, so the anti-smoking message applies to men too!

Diet

Certain foods or their lack have from time to time been considered as causes of miscarriage. There is increasing interest at the moment in the effects of diet on all sorts of illnesses and health, perhaps because this is an area over which we all have some control. Most people in Britain, Europe and the USA would seem to get a reasonable balance of nutrients in their everyday diet. Even those diets that do not fall in line with the particular present fashion or ideal (a low fibre diet, for example) have not been found to have any obvious effects on the incidence of miscarriage. Indeed, there is no conclusive evidence that any particular element of diet is involved in causing miscarriage. This includes tea and coffee. So far as vitamins are concerned, there is a suggestion that deficiency of folic acid may play a part – but there has really been very little work in this area on which any definite conclusions can be based.

Occupation

When one looks at variations between women in rates of pregnancy loss, a pattern of greater loss in certain socioeconomic groups is immediately apparent. Whether one is focussing on miscarriage, on pre-term labour, on congenitally malformed or low birthweight babies, or on perinatal mortality (the deaths of babies between 28 weeks of pregnancy and the end of the first week of life), the picture is still the same, and women who are most disadvantaged socially and economically are considerably more likely to have a poor outcome to their pregnancies.

Although this pattern is visible in the birth and death statistics of many countries, and has been found to exist ever since such statistics were first collected in the nineteenth century, we do not really know what it means. Most of the statistics divide women up into social 'classes' based on the work their husbands do. In Britain there are five such classes, going from social class I (professional) to social class V (unskilled manual workers). The reasons why husbands' occupations and not women's own occupations are used are mainly historical, and have to do both with the fact that women are more often not employed than men, and with the general belief that the way women live is shaped more by the men they live with than by women themselves.

The risk of a working-class woman miscarrying is probably about 50 per cent higher than that of a middle-class woman. The most likely explanation of the increased risk is that it is due to a combination of many factors – poorer diet in pregnancy and the mother's own childhood, more smoking, more arduous domestic work, and so on. While some of these factors on their own might not seem to enhance the risk of miscarriage, their combined effect may be a definite hazard to the pregnancy.

A woman wanting to avoid a repeat miscarriage clearly cannot just change her social class. However, there are two more specific groups of factors associated with parental occupation that we can be more precise about. The first is the physical and psychological effect of pregnant women's own work. The second group of factors are those direct chemical and other toxic effects associated with particular kinds of work. We will look at each of these in turn.

Work in pregnancy

About half of all pregnant women in Britain are in paid work during pregnancy. Between two thirds and three quarters are employed up to or beyond 28 weeks. Of course all women are also active throughout their lives in another area of work – domestic work, which for many, including many pregnant women, also embraces the care of children. Very little research has been done on the possible impact of housework and child care on chances of miscarriage or any other unsuccessful pregnancy outcome. This is because it's hard to get data on what women actually do in the home, and because the heritage of Victorian attitudes to women and work has meant that researchers have been more aware of the possible bad effects of employment than of its possible good effects (and they have not dwelt very much on the potential burden on pregnant women of housework, a socially acceptable female role).

So far as employment work is concerned, there is no evidence that being employed rather than not being employed makes miscarriage more likely. Some recent French research suggests that, overall, chances of successful pregnancy are higher in employed women – but this may be in part because certain kinds of women work in pregnancy (women suffering from illness, for example, are less likely to work). The French research did not look at miscarriage specifically, but rather at the incidence of babies born early, before 37 weeks of pregnancy. The findings here were that the following factors raised a woman's chances of giving birth early: a longer-than-average working week, working on an industrial conveyor belt, a job involving a lot of physical effort, one requiring little mental attention, an unpleasant working environment (noisy, cold, wet, etc.), and a long journey to work on public transport.

Stress

The idea that miscarriages are caused by stress is an old one. More than 250 years ago a doctor called James Blondel observed that the prosperity of the fetus in all senses depends upon that of the mother. Thus mental agitation, emotional disappointment, loneliness, boredom – all these could adversely affect the child in the womb. The remedy, not a bad one, was to give the mother anything she wants!

The word 'stress' comes from the same linguistic root as 'distress' and refers, according to the dictionary, to 'the overpowering pressure of some adverse force or influence'. One of the problems with the idea of stress as a cause of miscarriage is that an awful lot of different kinds of experience can be regarded as stressful. In what sense is it, then, helpful to say that 'stress' causes miscarriage? A second problem is that women looking back at the experience of miscarriage are more inclined to *remember* an apparently stressful event or period in their lives than if the miscarriage hadn't happened – but with a normal birth, the chain of events would have been the same, it just wouldn't have been given the same meaning.

Having said that, it is nonetheless true that there is a large amount of animal evidence, and a much smaller amount of evidence from studies with human beings, to suggest that a stressed or distressed mother is more likely to lose her fetus than one who is not stressed. This loss occurs both through miscarriage and by giving birth to a baby too early or too small for the baby to have a reasonable chance of survival. Some of the stresses experienced by mothers during pregnancy are not, of course, under their control; for example, deaths or illnesses in family or friends, unexpected unemployment, being made homeless and so forth. But inasmuch as different women react to life-stresses with different degrees of anxiety, it is possible to think of ways of making oneself less anxious (for example, by deliberately taking life as calmly as possible, not taking on too much work or a hectic social life, and so on). It is also quite possible that the seeming effectiveness of some of the treatments for miscarriage discussed in chapter 7 is not due to the treatment as such, but rather to the mother feeling less anxious because *something* is being done.

Toxic chemicals

Certain jobs a woman does during pregnancy may expose her and her fetus to known harmful substances. She or the fetus may also be exposed to these indirectly via the father's work. The list of different possible noxious agents is legion and we have confined ourselves to only two – anaesthetic gases and lead.

ANAESTHETICS

Some studies have shown an increased risk of miscarriage in those women who come into contact with anaesthetic gases in pregnancy, while others have not. The interpretation of the results of the various studies is made the more difficult as the dosage of exposure, maternal and/or paternal exposure, and the particular stage in the pregnancy or time before conception, have often not all been allowed for in the analysis. With this uncertainty, it is probably best to avoid exposure just before conception and in early pregnancy. Hospital staff working directly with anaesthetic gases or in operating theatres may be able to change their work in early pregnancy, or when anticipating pregnancy. So far as anaesthetics directly administered to pregnant women are concerned, these are only really needed in an emergency. It is sensible to avoid non-emergency operations early in pregnancy.

LEAD

Anxieties about exposure to lead, especially during pregnancy are not new – in the past, lead was deliberately used to produce abortions. Its effects in the sort of levels to which we are normally exposed or exposed at work are not clear, but recent studies have shown that miscarriage rates are increased in women exposed to lead through work or living near a lead smelter. Exposure to lead may also have some effect on the sperm, as rates of spontaneous abortion have been shown to be highest if both the mother *and* father are exposed to lead.

Irradiation

When X-rays were first discovered around the turn of the century their hazards were not understood, and so in some places they were used in an uncontrolled way during pregnancy – even to diagnose pregnancy (hormonal pregnancy tests didn't become available until much later, in the 1930s). The long-term problems associated with pregnancy X-rays didn't really become clear until the 1950s, when a report was published claiming higher rates of childhood cancer among children who had been X-rayed in their mothers' wombs. Since then there has been a sharp decline in the use of X-rays in pregnancy.

There is good animal evidence that irradiation produces chromosomal abnormalities and increased miscarriage rates. However, when the effects of irradiation on miscarriage rates have been looked at in women, the results are conflicting. Although there is no evidence that low doses of radiation cause miscarriage, in the 1920s large doses of irradiation were used deliberately to induce abortions in the early months of pregnancy in women with tuberculosis. In Hiroshima the effects of irradiation on fertility following the dropping of the bomb in 1945 have been studied, and while certain cancers have been shown to have increased, it has been difficult to demonstrate any pronounced effect on chromosomal abnormalities and miscarriage rates. Of course, this may in part be due to the difficulties in collecting the data.

Because of this general awareness of the dangers of irradiation, most women these days are not X-rayed in pregnancy unless it is unavoidable, e.g., if you break your leg. To avoid exposure to X-rays at the most sensitive stage of the baby's development immediately after conception when most women are unaware that they are pregnant, most radiologists avoid taking X-rays of women of childbearing age in the second half of their menstrual cycle unless the women are sure that they could not be pregnant. Similarly with dental X-rays, although there is no evidence that they cause miscarriage or other problems in pregnancy, it is best to avoid them while pregnant. Women whose work brings them into contact with radiation are usually encouraged to adopt protective screening in pregnancy, although this screening is not always used. We are thinking here not only of medical radiologists and radiographers but of women working with X-rays in industry to check metal equipment or at airports to examine baggage.

Ultrasound

Ultrasound is being used more and more in modern obstetrics. In some centres all women are routinely given an ultrasound at some stage during pregnancy, in other centres it is only used when there is a specific indication, e.g., to help locate the site of the placenta prior to amniocentesis; to monitor the baby's growth if there are anxieties that the baby is not growing at the right rate; to diagnose twins etc. To date, no maternal or fetal hazards of routine ultrasound screening have been reported. No association between ultrasound and miscarriage has been found in humans, but, on the other hand, there is animal evidence of ultrasound damage, so that long-term studies are still needed to help evaluate its ultimate safety in human pregnancy.

Drugs

Very little is known about the possible association between various drugs and miscarriage, because most of the research in this area has concentrated on looking at the effects of drugs taken in pregnancy on liveborn babies. A few drugs are known to increase miscarriage rates – for example certain drugs called anti-metabolites which are used in the treatment of cancer. There is no evidence that the commonly used drugs, such as aspirin, paracatemol, penicillin, etc., are associated with miscarriage, but it is obviously best to avoid taking any drug unnecessarily.

Immune mechanisms

Some kind of ill-defined immunological process has been suggested as a reason for miscarriage, especially among women having recurrent miscarriages. The body's immune system produces cells and chemical substances to protect against infection by isolating and rejecting from the body anything that is recognized as being 'foreign'. This usually works well when a bit of dirt or some bacteria get into the body. But the reaction is sometimes less desirable, for instance following a skin graft or a kidney transplant from one person to another. In these cases the receiving person's immune system tends to reject and kill off the transplant because the genetic material (genes and chromosomes) is not identical to that in the 'receiving' body. In order to overcome this problem it is possible to use powerful drugs which suppress the functioning of the immune system so that the graft is not rejected.

From the immunological point of view, pregnancy is interesting because the developing fetus and the half of the placenta that 'belongs' to the fetus 'ought' to be recognized as 'foreign' by the mother's body. The chromosomes are a new mix, and only half of them belong to the mother; the rest belong to the father and are 'foreign'. So why doesn't the mother's body produce cells and chemical substances to reject the foreign being – the developing baby? In order for the pregnancy to continue normally the usual immune system response of the mother must be controlled in some way. This importance of immunological factors in the maintenance of normal pregnancy suggests that the same factors could somehow be involved in miscarriage. However, this is a complex area and no one really has any answers as yet. For example, on the grounds of what we have said so far, you might suppose that the more alike the chromosomes of the mother and father, the more alike the total chromosomes of the baby will be to the mother, and so the *less* likely the mother's immune system will be to recognize and reject the fetus as being foreign. But actually the reverse is true: the *greater* the difference in the parents' genetic make-up and therefore the baby's, the *less* likely there is to be early recurrent miscarriage. Thus, it seems probable that, for a successful pregnancy, the mother's body actually has actively to recognize the fetus as being foreign in order to set in motion a special immune response which permits implantation and growth of the fertilized egg.

Another associated process is the production by the mother of 'blocking' factors. It is well recognized that the sera (blood from which the red cells have been removed) of pregnant women inhibit the rejection of foreign materials. According to present methods of testing, not all women have these blocking factors, and some women with recurrent miscarriages do lack them – although there are others who actually seem to have an *excess* of the factors. Trials are now being carried out in women who have recurrent miscarriages to try to promote the production of the blocking factors in women with low levels using special blood transfusion techniques. This treatment may be the answer for a small number of women with recurrent miscarriages, but it is not likely to be the answer for all such women. There are obviously even more complex factors than those outlined here which could explain a possible association between the immune system and recurrent miscarriage, but at the moment, and, as one expert in the field recently put it, 'The case for an immune cause of one kind or another remains valid, tantalizing, but unproven.'

Infections

Data showing any association between infection and spontaneous miscarriage are difficult to come by. For example, brucellosis is a well-recognized cause of miscarriage in animals, but there is no such clearcut association between infection and miscarriage in humans. It seems to be accepted in the medical literature that any generalized infection associated with high fever may lead to miscarriage. If fever does actually cause a miscarriage, it could either be due to biochemical change brought about by the fever, or it could be due to the direct effects of the infecting organism. There are certainly a number of organisms which are known directly to affect the developing fetus. These include rubella (german measles), cytomegalovirus, herpes, syphilis, toxoplasmosis; but although these produce abnormalities which are seen in the children once they are born, whether or not (or how often) the infections cause spontaneous miscarriage is not known.

Obviously in a general way it is a good idea, if you are pregnant, to avoid contact with someone known to have an infectious illness. On the other hand, it is impossible and silly to try to isolate yourself from everyone who *might* be infectious. Minor infections such as colds and brief flu-like episodes are not important, and the dangers of infectious illness in early pregnancy should not be allowed to get out of perspective. Other than rubella, the common childhood illnesses such as chickenpox, mumps, etc., appear themselves to pose no danger as far as miscarriage or the developing fetus are concerned.

Accidents

Falls and other accidents are often thought to be a cause of miscarriage (see chapter 5). However, we were unable to find any studies which looked specifically at this.

4 Having a Miscarriage

So far in this book we have looked in a general way at miscarriage, described the process of normal early pregnancy, and run through what is known about why miscarriages happen. In this chapter we look more closely at the experience of having a miscarriage. How do you know you are having a miscarriage? What is it that first alerts you to this possibility? How much pain and bleeding are normal? At what stage, and how, does it become clear that the loss of the baby is inevitable? What happens then? What sort of medical treatment do most women have – or should they have? These are some of the questions to which women commonly want to know the answer. Most of the answers we give in this chapter come from the accounts women sent us in our miscarriage survey. This has the advantage that what we are hearing about are the lived experiences of women rather than the descriptions offered in medical textbooks – which are not necessarily wrong, but are bound to be selective and based on doctors' views of the important things to mention in describing the process of miscarriage. Doctors' views are discussed later in chapter 9.

Signs and symptoms

In table 4.1 we have listed the 'symptoms' women in our questionnaire survey reported noticing first. By far the most common first sign of impending miscarriage was a coloured discharge or bleeding:

The day before the miscarriage, a brown discharge started.

The discharge was only slight, but on contacting my midwife, she sent me to bed for rest. I was thirteen weeks pregnant. (Elizabeth Woodward)

I started to lose fresh blood which got worse despite bedrest at home. (Ellen Cox)

Table 4.1 **First symptoms* of miscarriage**

	%	no.
Bleeding/discharge/spotting	67	(100)
Pain	15	(22)
Backache	3	(4)
Felt uneasy	10	(14)
Regression of pregnancy symptoms, e.g., breast tenderness, nausea	3	(4)
Told at clinic that baby not growing	1	(2)
Mother noticed self that uterus not enlarging after sixteenth week	1	(1)
Total	100	(147)

* Total number of symptoms mentioned

When pain was the first sign, various different sorts of pain were mentioned. Sally Howard described a 'bad stomach ache' early one morning; 'I felt like I was badly constipated, and went to the loo. Passed some blood.' Severe backache, bad enough to cause a woman to leave work or contact her GP, was also mentioned. Louise Godwin had both:

I was walking up a steep hill, taking the boys to school and playschool. It started on the way back, a pain in my stomach very low down and backache. I phoned the doctor, he said, 'just rest'. This was Monday. I lost the baby on Wednesday. I would have been seven weeks pregnant.

A woman who has not previously had a miscarriage doesn't know what to expect and may be slow to recognize that the miscarriage is underway. This is not to say, of course, that a woman having two or three miscarriages will have exactly the same experience each time. It's clear from the accounts women sent us that, even if all the miscarriages happen at roughly the same stage of pregnancy, the sequence of events can be quite different. One miscarriage may start with an intermittent brown discharge, one with fresh bleeding and another with cramp-like pains, for example. Nevertheless, it may be particularly hard to recognize what's going on if you've never miscarried before:

I felt the baby moving low down, and noticed a slight loss of fluid, but I didn't know any better, after reading it was common for pregnant women to have a discharge. This went on for two or three days until I noticed some blood, which prompted me to consult my doctor, who had me admitted to hospital.

Felicity Smith, who had a late miscarriage, wrote:

I had slight spotting very early on, but all settled down till 26 weeks. I began with contractions about 3.00 in the afternoon, but didn't realize what they were. I went to the doctor's, due to the severity of the pains, but was told I had a bladder infection and went to stay with my parents. At 2.00 in the morning my waters broke and then I knew something was wrong. I was taken to hospital, examined and told that it was too late to prevent the miscarriage. About 5.00 in the morning, the twins were born dead.

A late miscarriage is a mini-labour and most women, like Felicity, find it extremely distressing to have to go through labour knowing the baby (or babies in this case) are dead. Felicity said:

I didn't want to co-operate with my body. I was very depressed for about three months after, and even now, eight years and a perfect little boy later, I feel upset about it and think of them often.

More rarely a miscarriage can happen with scarcely any pain or bleeding. Ruth Barker, who was also expecting twins, described her experience at twenty weeks thus:

I started with what were like mild period pains which became worse over the next 10–12 hours. I had no bleeding until I had lost the first twin.

While contraction or period-type pains, backache, discharge and bleeding are sometimes signs of impending miscarriage, we feel it is important to point out that all these symptoms can occur in pregnancies that do not miscarry. We discuss bleeding in pregnancy in more detail later (pages 167–9). It should be remembered that, although most bleeding in early pregnancy comes from inside the womb where the placenta is joined to the wall of the womb, there are other possible, but uncommon, sources for the bleeding. These include an erosion or polyp of the cervix and lesions in the vagina. An internal examination with a speculum will help sort out where the bleeding is coming from.

One of the most interesting aspects of answers in our own survey to the question 'when did you first think something was wrong?' is the number of women who reported 'knowing' they would lose their pregnancies even before some definite physical sign:

I had had a funny feeling of being 'not quite right' throughout the day before and then that evening I started to lose blood. This was two days before the miscarriage. (Margaret Dwyer)

I felt terrible the day before. Had a very uneasy feeling and knew something had gone wrong. Next morning noticed slight bleeding but no pain. (Marie Farmer)

Immediately I sensed something was wrong and each time I bled early on, this seemed to confirm my thoughts – funnily enough on these occasions we told no one of the pregnancy, but when I was pregnant with my daughter, we did. That time I had no thoughts at all that anything would go wrong. (Julie Crawford)

It's difficult to know whether in these cases what women are responding to is some sort of ill-defined physical sign that all is not right with the pregnancy. Some also describe a general feeling of being unwell that is their first signal of threatened miscarriage:

With every one I woke up feeling sick and dizzy. I started losing blood the same day. With all but the first one I knew what to expect. (Eloise Robinson, four miscarriages at 8, 9, 12 and 26 weeks)

Others notice a definite regression of pregnancy symptoms: 'I didn't feel right. Breasts lost their 'tingly' feeling' (Rose Lerner) or:

I felt pregnant at about 5 weeks, but that feeling seemed to disappear and by 6–7 weeks I was becoming doubtful about my being pregnant. I felt uneasy about it, as I was not experiencing any nausea – I had been very sick whilst carrying my daughter. (June Thomas)

Christine Wainwright just noticed that at 15–16 weeks her uterus was no longer enlarging, and it took some time for her to persuade the hospital staff that something was wrong:

I mentioned it to the doctor at the clinic – he queried my dates. At my next antenatal appointment, he decided to repeat the pregnancy test and book me for a scan. At 21 weeks I was told the pregnancy had stopped growing . . . the consultant . . . believed in 'letting nature take its course' and I had to wait several weeks for the D & C. It was very distressing to know that I was carrying a dead baby.

Christine Wainwright's miscarriage was what is known as a 'missed abortion' in which the fetus fails to develop or dies and is only miscarried some time later. Having a missed abortion usually means that the symptoms of miscarriage are spread out over a period of weeks, or even months. It may be unclear whether the fetus is still alive or not: the best test is an ultrasound scan which can tell from early in the first three months whether the fetal heart is beating or not. Repeat scans can tell whether or not the fetus is continuing to grow. A rather extreme experience of missed abortion was described by Barbara Ford: we include it here because it illustrates well both the difficulty women may face in finding out whether the fetus is alive or dead, and the emotional trauma of not knowing if you are or are not pregnant.

I experienced a so-called 'missed abortion'. I had pains and bleeding at approximately three months but didn't pass the fetus until *seven months* later. At first my GP thought the baby would survive a 'threatened' miscarriage, but when a subsequent pregnancy test proved negative, he sent me to a specialist gynaecologist. She examined me internally and questioned me and decided that a D & C was not necessary as, in her opinion, there was no more to come away. Both she and my GP asked if I thought it had all come away, but I told them I could not tell, as I had not experienced a miscarriage before and did not know what to expect to pass. I had lost quite a lot of blood and clots over several days.

During the following months, I had no periods at all for five months followed eventually by more pains and bleeding as before, and then by several weeks of a brown discharge. I went back to my GP who arranged blood tests and urine tests, but could find nothing wrong. I was given distalgesic for the pain.

Eventually, on Boxing Day December 1979, I passed the fetus – it was about one and a half inches long and horribly mouldy – smelt terrible* . . . I couldn't face keeping it to show the doctor, so I flushed it down the toilet. I went back to my GP and told him what had happened. He still didn't think a D and C was necessary but that nature would take its course. He advised using contraception for a couple of months.

Several months later, I found I was pregnant again and went on to have a healthy daughter.

I still feel annoyed at those wasted seven months when I could have been trying to conceive again, and also the prolonged pain and inconvenience I suffered waiting for 'nature to take its course'. I feel that a D & C at the time of the miscarriage could have spared me all that.

What happens when you miscarry?

As the first signs and symptoms of threatened miscarriage vary, so there is tremendous variation between women in the overall experience of having a miscarriage. In our survey questionnaire we asked women to describe what happened during their miscarriage and we also asked them a number of specific questions. We asked if they saw a doctor, if they went into hospital, whether or not they had a D & C and whether they saw the fetus. Women's experiences of miscarriage are obviously partly shaped by their medical treatment. This is by no means uniform, as we show on pages 90–2 and in chapter 9, when we discuss the answers given by a small number of doctors to some questions we asked about their treatment of miscarriage.

* See page 95 for other similar observations.

Table 4.2 **Some aspects of the experience of miscarriage**

	% miscarriages*
Doctor contacted before completion of miscarriage	94
Hospital admission	78
D & C	72
Mother saw fetus	21

*Total number of miscarriages — 219

While the majority of women did contact a doctor during the miscarriage, about a quarter did not go into hospital or have a D & C. One in five fetuses were seen by their mothers. Whether or not a woman goes into hospital for her miscarriage appears to be influenced by a number of factors. (Once in hospital it is nearly always the case that a D & C will be done, as table 4.2 shows.) A D & C is done for many different reasons and is the most commonly performed gynaecological operation in this country. The reason why a woman having a miscarriage might be given a D & C is because fragments of tissue of the placenta and fetus (called in medical language, rather insensitively, the 'products of conception') may remain in the womb, causing prolonged and/or heavy bleeding and increasing the risk of infection. The procedure is carried out under anaesthetic, usually a general anaesthetic, so you are not conscious during the operation. Occasionally a local anaesthetic is used instead, and this has the advantage that you do not have the after-effects (sleepiness and sometimes nausea) of a general anaesthetic to contend with. For the actual operation, you lie on your back and your legs are put into 'stirrups' so that it is easier for the gynaecologist to do the operation. The vulva, vagina and cervix are cleaned with antiseptic, and a speculum (a metal instrument) is placed in the vagina to visualize the cervix. The cervix is held in place whilst the length of the uterus is measured with a small rod-like dilator. The cervix is then slowly widened using dilators of different widths. This has to be done gradually as the muscle in the cervix is tight and it is important not to stretch it so much that it gets torn (see chapter 7), yet sufficiently to allow the lining and contents of the womb to be gently scraped out using a curette. This removes any bits of placenta or fetus left inside.

It is unclear how many miscarriages really require hospital admission and a D & C, and the policies followed by different doctors are quite variable. Some GPs appear to send women to hospital almost immediately if a miscarriage is threatening. Other GPs will tell the woman to go to bed and rest and, if the symptoms have not abated within a few days, they will send her to hospital then. Some women may have a strong preference for or against hospital; quite commonly, after one or two miscarriages treated in hospital, a woman will choose not to go in the next time, particularly if she feels the miscarriage is a straightforward one. As with birth, there is a certain comfort to be derived from staying in your own home, and several of the women who completed our questionnaire mentioned this. Others, of course, gain a feeling of security from going into hospital. Occasionally, miscarriages are accompanied by very heavy bleeding and, in that case, a blood transfusion in hospital may be needed.

Very little is known about how GPs decide what to do in cases of threatened miscarriage – or what most of them decide (see chapter 9). One of the consequences of the relative lack of interest shown by the medical profession over the years in the subject of miscarriage is that we also do not know what is the best form of treatment for threatened or inevitable miscarriage. The most commonly recommended 'treatment' in our survey, bedrest, is discussed in chapter 7 which deals with the question of treatment in general. (Often bedrest is not first suggested by the GP but is the woman's response to the sign that all may not be well with the pregnancy – 'I went to bed and rested immediately.') Because of the lack of research it is also unclear as to how many women having miscarriages really benefit from a D & C. Some doctors have a prejudice in favour of 'letting nature take its course' as we saw in Christine Wainwright's case earlier. Yet others believe that, so long as there is conclusive evidence of no live fetus, a D & C may as well be done straight away and that all women having miscarriages should have a D & C to avoid any possible risk of excess bleeding or infection. Whether or not a D & C is done may also depend on whether there is evidence that the miscarriage is complete or not. If the doctor has reason to believe it is incomplete, he or she is more likely to recommend a D & C to avoid any complications.

In deciding whether or not to do a D & C, doctors are likely in the future to rely more and more on the use of good ultrasound to establish quickly and easily whether the fetus is dead, or whether there is just an empty sac in the uterus with no properly developing fetus at all. If there is no live fetus, then most doctors would not wait before doing a D & C.

The absence at present of uniform guidelines as to what should be done medically during and after miscarriage is responsible for some of the variation in experiences of the women in our survey. Sarah Fenton describes her three miscarriages:

Pregnancy was confirmed and at about seven weeks I started to have a pink discharge. The doctor was not concerned and told me to stay in bed till it stopped. I did for a week and then started having pains (like contractions). I woke up in the night and had bled very heavily. I lost a great deal of blood in the toilet and did actually see the fetus – it was a kind of bubble of transparent material. This was a Saturday. I saw a doctor on the Monday who simply asked if I'd gone to hospital. When I said 'no' he said 'Oh well, I'll give you a week off work. What shall I put on the certificate – stomach ache?' Nothing else was said.

The second time, she didn't even see the doctor:

The second time I had had a coil fitted. I knew I was pregnant but didn't see the doctor . . . I bled for about three or four weeks and then lost it. It wasn't as bad as the first time and I never saw the doctor as it didn't seem worth it.

The third time:

I had my coil removed – it was the middle of the month. The doctor asked if we'd had sex within the previous few days (we had) and he then said there was a possibility I could be pregnant. It turned out I was. My period was over two weeks late and a test was positive, although I had a slight pink/brown discharge. Over the next two weeks it stopped and started, and a second test at nine weeks was positive and I stopped bleeding for a fortnight. At eleven weeks it started again. I stayed in bed or lying down for a week (the doctor told me this was all that could be done). On 1 July I had an antenatal appointment at the hospital (I was twelve weeks then) and although I was bleeding much more I kept the appointment. The consultant examined me and said, 'Well, you're not pregnant anymore, have a scan to confirm it, and we'll keep you in hospital and take "it" away.' I stayed in and had an evacuation that night.

The first miscarriage happened quickly, although the lead-up to it was gradual, and since Sarah saw the fetus she felt relatively confident that the miscarriage was over. The second and third miscarriages were associated with the coil and were accompanied by prolonged bleeding, but only one of these took her into hospital – via the antenatal clinic.

The process of 'having a miscarriage' is sometimes complicated by uncertainty about the diagnosis of pregnancy. Lesley Anderson is a staff midwife:

When I was seven weeks I started to have a brown discharge but a pregnancy test was negative, and when I went to my GP he said that I wasn't pregnant and that it was the beginning of a late period, although I was feeling very sick. He sent me home with some iron tablets saying I was a bit anaemic. I had been trying to get pregnant for six months and was hoping very much to get pregnant, so he said that I was having myself on a bit.

I was working on a labour ward at the time, and while I was in theatre during a caesarean section a few days after seeing my GP, I started to get period-type pains. I didn't think much about it at the time because I thought it was just a late period starting properly. Then half an hour later I started bleeding quite heavily and went to the toilet and lost several large clots. I was examined internally and it was found that I had been pregnant and had just had a miscarriage. Then I was referred to a gynaecological ward for a D & C.

Afterwards she felt angry with her GP who she felt had 'fobbed her off' with iron tablets when she had stressed that she felt pregnant and had never had irregular periods starting with a brown discharge before. The post-miscarriage depression was cured only by the onset of the next pregnancy, which at the time of writing had reached 22 weeks and had included hospitalization for bedrest at six and ten weeks as well as hormone tablets.

Being in hospital during the early stages of a threatened miscarriage doesn't necessarily make things easier in the sense of enabling women to know exactly what is going on inside their bodies. When Marie Farmer was in hospital:

Every morning a urine test was taken to determine a count of (HCG?).* A scan at 10.30 a.m. revealed I had lost the baby, and I was not allowed lunch and booked for theatre that evening. However, at 2.30 p.m. having been upset for four hours, I was told everything was OK as my count was positive. For four days I was told OK by one person, only to have a nil by mouth card on my bed just in case the

* See page 52.

afternoon's result was negative. In the end, it was a relief to be taken to theatre – at least I knew that it was over. I felt at the time that I never wanted to try again for a baby – but eight months later I did, and now have a lovely daughter.

'Is the fetus really dead?' is one question. 'Have I really miscarried it?' is another:

I started bleeding (at twelve weeks) on the Thursday and stayed in bed. A doctor (not my own GP) came out to see me and with only an external examination said that he didn't think I'd lose the baby as I wasn't having any contractions.

I stayed in bed on Friday, and on Friday afternoon I started having strong pains. I found this more painful than period pains or labour pains. When I got up later there was a gush and various lumps came away – I thought I had aborted there and then.

Later in hospital the gynaecologist said that I was either aborting or had aborted. I was confined to bed.

I was overwhelmed by the smell of what was coming away. It smelt dead. I realized now that the baby had died earlier that week when I lost breast tension and generally stopped feeling pregnant.

I said I was sure I had lost the baby, but the nursing sister said, 'There's something you haven't told me: you haven't lost it.' I felt bewildered. I *knew* there was no hope.

Next morning, Saturday, they took a urine sample for a pregnancy test. I was bleeding heavily now and asked what was the point. I had strong pains for about an hour on Saturday morning. The pregnancy test was positive. I was more confused. After lunch I felt I wanted to open my bowels. Nothing happened. I asked to be sat on the pan on a chair and left alone. I sat and pushed and out popped a large ball of meat. God – how it stank. The nurse came and took it away. The sister came back – yes, I had miscarried. 'You can cry now,' she said. I couldn't.

The doctor came and told me I was to have a scrape. The neck of the womb was well open so I went to theatre at 6 p.m. I was awake by 6.30 p.m. There was no discomfort and very little bleeding. (Georgia Davies)

Some miscarriages take a long time, others are over quickly. Neither the physical nor the emotional trauma are related to the length of time a miscarriage takes. As table 4.2 shows, one in five fetuses were seen by their mothers. Some women were clear that they didn't wish to see the fetus: on the other hand, none of those who did see it regretted having done so, and a number who didn't made comments of the following kind:

'No, but I asked.'
'No, but I wanted to.'
'I was told not to look, but now I really wish I had.'
'On the scan I saw it – I was very upset, as it made the baby look even more real.'

Many women observe that the process of grieving for the lost baby is made harder by the sense of unreali surrounding a fetus expelled into a lavatory bowl and flushed away or taken away in a hospital bedpan to be incinerated. Some women expel the fetus from their bodies alone at home.

I was in bed and had bad pains as if it was labour. My waters broke and then I lost the baby. I had to take the baby away and cover it myself until the ambulance men arrived. (Gloria Watson)

Insofar as what is mourned after a miscarriage is a person, women must mourn a person usually of unknown sex that they have neither seen nor officially named. 'I was very confused,' said one woman whose miscarriage happened at fourteen weeks, 'that I never saw the baby or knew what it meant.' Hilary Evans found a painful solution to this problem:

> was only seven weeks when I lost the baby, but because keep a temperature chart I knew from the very moment hat my period was overdue that I was pregnant. My body lso promptly reacts to pregnancy with immediate changes o the breasts and sickness. Although this was a very early niscarriage, there was no way I could dismiss it as an overdue period, and not feel that the tiny foetus which I escued from the loo and we buried in the garden was not ny baby.

e further on in pregnancy a woman is when she miscarries, t more likely she is to need to conceptualize the fetus as a person in order to mourn it. Thus Felicity Smith, whose ins were born dead at 26 weeks, said:

> I have nothing to remind me of them but memories . . . My parents asked to see the twins but were refused, and I was too upset to even think about it at the time. I also wish they could have been buried instead of incinerated.

nother mother, Anna Wheeler, who miscarried at 23 eeks, although, strictly, the fetus was born alive, echoed ese feelings when she said:

> I feel it is very important to see the baby and I'm very regretful that I didn't. After the birth one is not emotionally 'with-it' enough to ask to see the baby. I was not offered the possibility, as the baby was whisked away to the Special Care Baby Unit where he survived for half an hour, and I was taken for the D & C immediately.

These experiences highlight the point we made in chapter 1 that medico-legal definitions of what constitutes a miscarriage as opposed to a stillbirth frequently do not correspond to women's own feelings: what is defined as a 'spontaneous abortion' may well be experienced as a birth. In these circumstances, women are inclined to welcome anything that puts them in touch with the reality of their baby – Denise Mitchell's 'spontaneous abortion' at 25 weeks was at almost the same stage as Felicity Smith's:

> When the baby was born he was alive and lived for forty minutes. During that time everything they did for the baby was done in the labour suite, which was nice as we were kept well informed.

Attitudes of medical staff and others

The way other people behave to women having miscarriages can hardly turn a bad experience into a good one, but it can certainly lessen the negative side of miscarriage. It's already obvious from many of our quotations from the survey material how important the attitudes of GPs and hospital staff are in shaping the experience of miscarriage. As we say in appendix I, our survey was not carried out on a random sample of women, and so may contain a higher proportion of women dissatisfied with their medical care than is representative of all women having miscarriages. This is because dissatisfied patients tend to air their complaints more readily than satisfied patients give their reasons for being satisfied. Nevertheless, there were many congratulatory comments about medical and nursing staff in our completed questionnaires. Table 4.3 puts these in the context of all answers to the question we asked about social support during and following miscarriage: 'Who was most helpful to you?'

Table 4.3 'Who was most helpful to you?'

	%
Husband	25
Mother (or mother-in-law)	6
Other relatives (including children)	5
Friend*	13
GP	17
Nurse†	13
Hospital doctor	8
Others (including God, chaplain, ambulance men and books)	5
No one	8
Total of 'helpful' people mentioned	100

*Often another woman who had had a miscarriage, or the woman in the next bed.

†Nurses on night duty and auxiliary nurses were particularly mentioned.

Husbands came top of the list, but GPs came second. Hospital doctors, by contrast, are mentioned as helpful only half as often and, indeed, come top of the list of the 'unhelpful' people mentioned by the women in our survey. (Although not specifically asked for, a number of women singled out unhelpful people in their answers.)

Table 4.4. 'Unhelpful' people

	%
Hospital doctor	48
GP	33
Nurse	7
Family/friends	9
Workmates	3
Total of 'unhelpful' people mentioned	100

Where medical staff were identified as unhelpful this was most often because of the way the staff behaved in general or because of something that was said. In most cases the underlying problem, which we discuss more fully in chapter 9, is that medical staff do not sufficiently appreciate that, while miscarriage may be a minor event medically, it may be a major event for the woman undergoing it. It is thus not enough for the treatment to be clinically good, as Pat Lawton points out:

The medical side of my induced labour was efficient to a point and success was achieved, but, my God, can't they just wait and think to themselves, this is a woman here who has just lost a baby: we should be a little bit sympathetic and think before we speak. Most of my doctors were men. Perhaps that is why they behaved like they did. I had eighteen hours of severe labour pains brought on by a drip and some tube inserted into my womb which they pumped fluid into. This inflated and so stimulated labour. The attitude of the doctors was unbelievable at times. At one point I was told that the pain isn't so bad – as if he would bloody know.

More often it is a general lack of consideration for a woman's feelings or a curtly dismissive attitude:

The consultant came to see me 48 hours after I was admitted, along with about six students, and talked to me in a four-bed ward from the middle of the room. How could I tell him my feelings and fears, and discuss what might happen?

When I visited my doctor after coming out of hospital, I felt like it was the end of the world and all he said was – 'so you lost the baby did you' like it was a bus ticket or something.

In only a few cases there was a blatant lack of sympathy for the mother's point of view. A Catholic woman who had had five miscarriages (and had three living children) describes what is fortunately (as judged by our limited survey) a rare experience in her last, early pregnancy:

The consultant informed me I wasn't pregnant. I said I was. He said he'd been in the business thirty years and I wasn't. I said he might have been, but it was the eighth time I'd been pregnant and he'd never felt what it was like to be pregnant in his life.

Then a woman doctor who I'd had dealings with before walked in and said without caring, 'I see someone hasn't taken any contraceptive advice then.' I was livid. I am a Catholic, and for all she knew I had been trying to become pregnant. Even the consultant was shocked. This comment has never left me.'

There were few complaints about the technical standard of medical treatment in hospital. Many women who went on to have a successful pregnancy only after intensive medical care could not say enough about the excellence of that care and the support of those who provided it. A message that emerged clearly from this part of the survey is that some women have to 'shop around' a fair bit among NHS hospitals and consultants (and sometimes private ones as well) to find the sort of care they are happy with.

It would be fair to say that a valid conclusion from our survey is that considerate treatment from medical staff, family and friends helps women to go through the experience of miscarriage with a minimal level of distress. In the next chapter we examine in more detail the psychological and emotional impact of miscarriage and the communication and support needed as women attempt to make sense of their experience of miscarriage.

5 Adjusting to Miscarriage

We have called this chapter 'Adjusting to Miscarriage' because it covers a number of topics to do with events and processes following miscarriage. We will discuss in turn what we called in chapter 1 the 'why me?' syndrome – women's search for explanations as to why the miscarriage happened; the impact of cultural attitudes generally on women's recovery from miscarriage; different strategies of coping after miscarriage; some of the ways in which the experience of miscarriage may affect people's relationships; and, lastly, practical questions about the physical aftermath of miscarriage which women frequently do not feel able to ask doctors (or doctors do not have the time or inclination to answer). We have put all these topics under the heading of 'Adjusting to Miscarriage' because they concern the social and personal significance of miscarriage, and the attempt to 'make sense' of miscarriage as an unplanned and untoward event which, nevertheless, becomes accommodated as a meaningful and bearable part of our histories. This is the sense in which we use the term 'adjustment'.

For some women miscarriages are never forgotten completely. What we have learnt from the descriptions women sent us of their miscarriages is just how much the experience of miscarriage may remain vividly and easily remembered, even many years later. On the other hand, for some women the experience may be completely superseded by the birth of later children, and never thought about again. These women are, of course, less likely to respond to a questionnaire survey about miscarriage:

It was only when my friend had a miscarriage in her first

pregnancy and was very upset by it that I remembered my own miscarriages. I had two of them – six and eight years ago – and had not thought of them since. The first one happened when my first child was two, and I had decided to have another baby. I was very excited when I realized I was pregnant, and at the time upset when I started to bleed just after I knew I was pregnant, around six weeks. I was worried that there was something wrong with the baby, and felt I wanted to miscarry as quickly as possible, if there was any risk of this. I miscarried that night, did not call my doctor, and got pregnant again three months later.

The second miscarriage occurred after my second child. This time I was twelve weeks pregnant, and I was much more upset, as I was beginning to allow myself to believe in the pregnancy, although it hadn't been planned (it was a cap failure). My husband was also very upset by the miscarriage, but found it difficult to talk about it.

As soon as I miscarried, I wanted to get pregnant again and did so. After I passed the twelve-week stage when my previous miscarriage had occurred, I stopped worrying about having a miscarriage, but only worried that the baby would be normal (as I did in all my pregnancies). She was, and my husband and I have never talked about the miscarriage since. I certainly never thought of the miscarriages as potential people.

To illustrate many of the key themes of this chapter, we continue with an account sent to us by Dorothy Alexander, who had a missed abortion in her first pregnancy and actually had labour induced at 24 weeks. Dorothy was one of the many women who observed that being given the chance to write down in detail her feelings about miscarriage was a positive help. Dorothy wrote:

It has helped me enormously to tell you all about it and hopefully for you to have got some use from my experience. I feel as if I have now done all I can for my dead baby, and I can finally put it to rest.

I thought I had got over it until I found myself . . . telling my story and crying . . . as I relived it . . . I have kept a copy in case I should ever need it, perhaps for my future daughter if the same thing happens to her!

It's very hard to know where to begin. I started my periods when I was thirteen and they were always regular and trouble free. I have never had any serious illnesses and my gynaecological history is completely normal. I went on the pill when I was sixteen as I had been going steady with David (who I later married) since I was fourteen. I attended clinic regularly for checks and had regular smears. Everything was normal. We had been married for two years and decided we wanted to start a family, so I came off the pill in December 1980 (I'd been on the pill just five years) . . . I got pregnant straightaway.

It came as a bit of a shock, as I'd thought it would take a few months and I'd heard it wasn't wise to get pregnant immediately after coming off the pill. I mentioned my fears to several doctors and nurses but they all said that was nonsense. When I was a week late I did a home pregnancy test which was positive, so I went to the doctor and he did a test too. I was thrilled to be pregnant as I wanted a large family and all I ever really wanted from life was to be a wife and mother. I immediately stopped drinking any alcohol *at all* (I hardly ever drank anyway), took no medicines (not even aspirin), watched my weight, took it easy and ate good foods. I read lots of baby books and watched every TV programme about babies and pregnancy. I wanted to do everything I could for the coming baby. I felt very well – I had very little morning sickness, but felt very tired so I rested accordingly. I carried on working in the office but told them I would be leaving eleven weeks before the baby was due, so they started training an office junior to take my place. We collected a few things for the baby, but no major items like prams etc. I was very happy to be pregnant, but I think I took it all for granted – it had been so easy to get pregnant. I attended all my antenatal checkups and I was fine every time. I had no oedema, my blood pressure and weight were normal, but it was found I had rhesus negative blood. I was tested early on for antibodies and was told I would have another test later on in my pregnancy. The baby grew normally but was always a little large for dates. However, I was sure of my dates and 'large-for-dates' babies are normal in our family. I am like my mum and grandma with large bones and all the babies on both sides of the family were usually nine pounders.

I first felt the baby kick at about 18–19 weeks and by 22 weeks it was kicking very strongly and actively. That was when I began to get rather fond of it – it was becoming a baby in my mind rather than a pregnancy . . . At about 19 weeks I went for a checkup and the doctor again said the baby was large-for-dates, so if I was still large next time he would send me for a scan to assess my dates. I knew my dates were right and thought, great, the baby's thriving and I felt OK to go on holiday to Wales a week or so later. We drove down and the baby seemed particularly lively on the journey, beginning just before I got into the car. It was still kicking when we got there. I didn't enjoy the holiday much, for some reason I felt very, very depressed and tired. We were busy sightseeing that week, so towards the end of the week I realized with a shock that I hadn't felt the baby kicking lately – in fact I wasn't sure just when I *had* last felt it. I got an awful uneasy feeling, and I felt very guilty that I hadn't noticed when it had stopped . . . I began to keep really still for long periods of time, trying to feel a tiny kick . . . Part of me kept thinking I was all right as long as I had no pain or bleeding – I had heard that sometimes babies stop moving for long periods of time and are perfectly all right after, and I knew this to be true because my baby had stopped for nearly a day round about the twentieth week. But this was more than a day . . .

By now, we were home from holiday and back at work and still the baby hadn't kicked . . . I started looking at myself in the mirror, waiting for the signs of pregnancy to disappear. I examined every vein on my breasts. Did they

seem less apparent? Was my tummy getting smaller? I
hounded David, who couldn't see any difference – all he
could say was, go to the doctor if you are worried.
Worried? I was almost out of my mind! Finally, after
nearly a week since I had felt the baby, I looked in the
mirror and there was a difference (at least I thought there
was). I went to pieces. It was early Saturday morning, I
woke David and he was wonderful to me. He calmed me
down as best he could – I was almost hysterical. Now I
knew I *had* to go to the doctor's. I had got to the point
where no matter what the doctor said it couldn't be any
worse than what I was already thinking.

This stage, when you do not know for certain what has
happened to the fetus and whether or not you will miscarry,
is an 'in-limbo' state. After days of having different people
listening on different machines for her baby's heartbeat,
Dorothy was eventually told that her baby was definitely
dead.

A very nice matronly nurse came to talk to me when I got
back from the scan. She asked me how old I was and when
I told her she said, 'Oh there's plenty of time for you yet.'
She said she bet I'd be back in the maternity ward in twelve
months with a new baby (as it happened it was thirteen and
a half months). I was told my miscarriage was just a fluke
of nature and there was very little chance of it happening
again (working on the 'lightning striking twice' theory),
but I couldn't see how they could say that when they didn't
know what had caused it. I really hoped they would find
something wrong with the baby, and then the miscarriage
would be justified in some way, but they never did. My
greatest comfort was thinking about the next baby and
planning ahead. If I had been told I couldn't have any
more children I think I would have gone totally to pieces.
As it was I think I coped very well, but I know if I hadn't
been able to think of the next one whenever I got depressed
I would have taken it far, far worse. As you can imagine,

with this frame of mind, my first priority was to get rid of the dead baby so I could begin trying for another straight away. It was not that I didn't care about the baby I had lost, but once I knew there was no hope, there wasn't any point in my carrying it around any longer. My love was for the baby I had already lost, I didn't think of the dead fetus as my baby any longer. My baby was gone already – the thing I was carrying was like a waste product which had to be 'disposed of' so that I would be capable of having another child. From then on until he was finally born, I referred to the next pregnancy as MK2 – new improved version – and funnily enough, when he was born we named him Mark!

Following induction of labour Dorothy delivered the baby into a bedpan; she didn't want to look at it, but she did want to know the sex.

They said it was a little girl. Once I knew the sex it became a real person – a baby, not just a 'pregnancy', and it really hurt because I had very much wanted a girl all along . . .

In a lot of ways I thought of the miscarriage like a death in the family and I have my own way of getting over something like bereavement – I prefer to cry my tears in private. On the surface I was almost normal, just a bit depressed, but now and then I would burst into tears or snap at David and I was letting my sadness out bit by bit. I preferred to keep the door of my room closed for the first few days so I could grieve in private, but the nurses said I should be more sociable, and seemed worried that I was shutting myself away like a hermit (I just wanted to be left alone so I wouldn't have to put on a brave face and could cry a bit) so we played 'musical doors' for a few days until I was ready to face the world again.

My greatest worry now and for the next few weeks was that someone would ask me about my pregnancy, not realizing I had lost the baby, but thanks to David and my family I was shielded from that. By the time I was out of hospital they had told everyone and I am eternally grateful for that because it made the whole ordeal so much easier for me . . .

When my milk came in, that really upset me. I had thought once the birth was over I could begin to forget the baby and look forwards, but this reminded me all over again. It really bothered me that I was overflowing with milk and had no baby to feed. It was like an extra turn on the thumbscrew . . . I told a Sister before I was discharged, but she said they wouldn't give me anything as she believed natural remedies are best. She told me to take Epsom salts when I got home and I would be OK . . . I took Epsom salts until it was coming out of my ears but all I got was diarrhoea! I suffered it for about five days but my breasts became engorged and very, very painful. I couldn't express the milk to relieve myself because that would make it worse. It became so bad I could hardly move – every step was painful and my breasts were leaking so I was all wet and sticky. My breasts felt like rocks and I was thoroughly miserable. Finally I could stand it no longer so I walked into the doctor's surgery and told the receptionist loudly what was the matter, demanding something to help me. (This is not characteristic of me at all!) The waiting-room was full and all the patients could hear but I didn't care. I was given some white tablets and within a day I was almost back to normal. I wondered why I couldn't have had the tablets in hospital and been saved the extra distress (see page 130).

From the day of the birth it was two steps forward and one back. I came out on Sunday and David had the following week off work to stay with me, but I was secretly quite glad when he went back to work so I could begin to get things back to normal. The week after I came out we had a new washing machine delivered and that same night it sprang a leak and we woke up to find all the downstairs of our house two inches deep in water. It didn't bother me one bit! I mopped it all up and sorted out the washer repair man and insurance man without batting an eyelid. I think the miscarriage has helped me to see things in their proper perspective. I used to fuss over the smallest things, but now nothing like that bothers me at all. I believe I have grown up a lot because of what happened to me, and I hope I am a better person for it.

David had been advised to hide all the baby things we had collected so I wouldn't see them when I got home, but luckily he knew better than that and he left everything as it had been when I left. I couldn't have borne it if he had taken away all the baby things . . . Although I wasn't even pregnant yet, it made the new baby seem so much closer if I could do things for it, so I carried on knitting and bought some bits and pieces. I joined a slimming club and lost my two surplus stones which I thought was probably the best thing I could do for my next baby at that time. All these things seemed a bit eccentric to some people who seemed to think I hadn't accepted the death of MK1, but doing things for MK2 really helped me come to terms with my miscarriage.

I had to see my doctor when I got out of hospital so I asked him if I could go back to work soon. He said it was up to me and I could have several weeks off if I wanted, but I didn't want to be on my own to brood any longer, and I thought the time would pass more quickly if I was busy, so I went back to work two weeks after leaving hospital. It was a bit awkward, because they had been training a girl to do my job and she had been looking forward to the promotion, but we were good friends so she understood, and I assured her that if I had my way she would be taking over from me very soon!

Once I was back at work I felt better. Most people treated me as if nothing had happened, which was the best thing, because someone came up to me and said how sorry he was to hear about the baby and I nearly burst into tears! A couple of weeks after leaving hospital I got my holiday photos back from the printers and cried for ages because I was pregnant in them. I went shopping with my mum and little sister. My mum wanted to go to Mothercare and asked me if I would be all right. I said yes, because I thought I could handle it. I picked up a pack of nappies which I wanted to buy for MK2 but my mum told me not to because I wasn't even pregnant yet, and it would be a very long time before I needed them. This upset me terribly and it was a struggle not to start crying. Then I came across a shelf full of first-size baby things. Then a rack of little dresses and it was just too much for me. Everywhere I looked there were baby clothes, which seemed to be almost mocking me, and I felt out of place in the shop because I was not pregnant and didn't have any children. I went and stood in a corner of the shop while I waited for my mum so that no one would see me . . . My mum was very sympathetic, and said, 'Well, you're not as tough as you seem, are you?' and I realized that, by hiding my feelings, it must have seemed as if I didn't care . . . Before I had the miscarriage I had imagined what it would be like and it was really not as bad as I had thought it would be. Of course it hurt – it still hurts to think of it sometimes – but it was bearable and I never felt like suicide or anything . . . But I don't like to think that anyone thought of me as hard and unfeeling when *inside* I was crying all the time.

In recovering from a miscarriage there will be emotional ups and downs, and the downs are likely to be precipitated by news of other people's pregnancies and babies and by special 'family' occasions such as Christmas. Dorothy Alexander, for example, recalled meeting her sister-in-law, who had conceived about the same time as her, at a family wedding.

We had joked of how we two would be trundling down the aisle together, so I had been dreading the wedding. The sister-in-law arrived 39 weeks pregnant and was very good in that she never spoke about her baby while I was within earshot and never even flinched when it kicked her hard which I thought was very considerate, although I probably wouldn't really have minded if she had. I managed to appear normal for most of the day, but by teatime the strain was too much and I am ashamed to say I burst out crying in front of all the guests at the barbecue, but I pulled myself together again after about half an hour and joined the party. David's mum wanted to know what was wrong with me – it hadn't occurred to her that I was crying about the baby, because the miscarriage had been two months before and she thought I had got over it. The week after, the sister-in-law had her baby. Thankfully it was a boy. If it had been a girl it would have upset me even more. The proud father rang us first which I thought was really nice. It was 11 p.m. and David answered the phone. I could tell by the conversation what it was about and when David said: 'Congratulations Daddy' with a break in his voice, I could have curled up and died . . .

At this time I counted a total of thirteen women I knew who were expecting (Lady Di had just announced her pregnancy). I did become rather obsessed with pregnancy. I was never very bothered by babies in prams, but if I saw a pregnant woman I became really depressed. I suppose if I had had a stillbirth or cot death it would have been the other way around. The only dresses I liked in shop windows were maternity dresses and I could spot a pregnant woman at a considerable distance although I am short-sighted and David didn't even notice her!

Our sex life suffered. I began to think of sex as just a way to get pregnant and nothing more. I was only really interested on the 'right' days of the month. David must have really suffered in lots of ways but he never complained and was a tremendous support to me through it all – when I got pregnant and felt happy again David sank into the blackest depression which lasted several weeks, and he must have been saving his own sadness until I was better again. What we went through could easily have broken up our marriage, but we got through it all and we are really happy now . . .

Christmas was another landmark. The Christmas before, I had vowed never to spend another Christmas without children and I had got pregnant shortly after. I had been very much looking forward to having a baby this year. Everything about Christmas made me cry. Christmas carols, the church services, the crib, my little sister's dancing school show with all the little children. I started to cry at the tiniest thing, even Christmas films with a happy ending. I couldn't avoid my sister-in-law any longer and I cried for hours after seeing her five months pregnant. I didn't drink any of the Christmas cheer 'just-in-case' and our house seemed really bleak and miserable even with all the decorations and the tree up. On the whole, it was a very sad Christmas and New Year, but it needn't have been because, although I didn't know it at the time, I was already pregnant, so it was just as well I hadn't drunk any alcohol. I discovered I was pregnant on 5 January, and have never looked back. My son was born in August.

Nobody has been able to give me a reason for the miscarriage. Perhaps it was with being on the pill so long, or getting pregnant so soon after coming off it? I wouldn't think so because the pregnancy was normal until 22 weeks. The doctors and nurses said it may have been the placenta which packed up, but why? There must have been a reason which caused it to suddenly fail. Could it have been a kink in the cord? Could it have been caused by the car journey or the holiday? Would it have helped if I had gone to a doctor immediately I realized the baby had stopped kicking? Would it have helped if the doctors and nurses had been quicker to act when I went to them? Was God punishing me for not loving the baby enough? Was it his way of showing me just how special each child is? I certainly don't take pregnancies and babies for granted any more. I believe each child is a privilege and should be thought of as the special gift which he is.

Whatever medical reason there was for the baby dying, I believe it was *meant* to be. That there was some special reason for it. Perhaps my changed attitude to life and children was the only reason? Perhaps Mark will grow up to do something miraculous for the world and he would never have been born if MK1 had lived . . .

Not every woman would reach the same conclusion as Dorothy Alexander, that her miscarriage is somehow *meant* to be. But, equally, it is very difficult to be satisfied with the idea that miscarriage is merely a biological accident. Some of the other common themes raised in her account are: the expectation many young women today have that the planning of families is totally within their control; the overwhelming and unreasonable guilt many feel when a pregnancy goes wrong; the very important supportive role of husbands – who nevertheless may need themselves also to be supported in recovering emotionally from miscarriage; miscarriage as bereavement, a 'death in the family'; the difficulty of facing the world after miscarriage; the ability of apparently small episodes to trigger major emotional distress even many months after miscarriage; the added trials of producing milk for a baby who isn't there; the extraordinary sensitivity to other people's pregnancies that often develops post-miscarriage; and, finally, the positive side of miscarriage as what psychologists would call a 'growth' experience. Death and disaster, whether major or minor, are a part of adult life, and it is a task of adulthood to develop the resources needed to confront problems without being permanently overcome by them.

Why me?

We asked the women who filled in our questionnaire what they thought had caused their miscarriages: the answers are given in table 5.1.

Table 5.1 **What do you think caused your miscarriage?**

	% women mentioning
Abnormal fetus	19
Illness/accidents/medication in early pregnancy	11
Overdoing it (e.g., moving house)	11
Hormone imbalance	10
Incompetent cervix	5
The pill (taking it 'too long', getting pregnant 'too soon' after stopping it)	5
The coil (became pregnant with it in place)	3
Placental insufficiency	3
Shock, worry, etc.	3
Getting pregnant too soon after baby/miscarriage	2
Sexual intercourse	1
Age	1
Blighted ovum	1
Antepartum haemorrhage*	1
Don't know	23
Total	100

*Bleeding occurring during pregnancy, after 28 weeks.

While about a quarter of the women said they didn't know the cause, three-quarters felt they could identify a factor or factors that could have contributed to the miscarriage. The most common was an abnormal fetus. Next in the list came some untoward event of early pregnancy – illness, falling downstairs, taking drugs of one kind or another (in most cases these were drugs prescribed by a doctor), or generally 'overdoing it' physically. One in ten women gave 'hormonal imbalance' as an explanation, and a smaller number mentioned an incompetent cervix and the contraceptive pill as precipitating factors. Of course there was usually no firm evidence for these 'causes' – rather, they were explanations which 'made sense' to the women concerned. The explanations may have been suggested by medical staff: 'abnormal fetus' came into this category, though it seemed to make more sense to women having their first experience of miscarriage than it did to those who had miscarried before. In other cases the 'cause' identified by the woman was suggested by her personal experience of the pregnancy. For example, 'hormonal imbalance' was cited as a reason for miscarriage by several women who had simply not 'felt pregnant' in the miscarried pregnancy, while they had done so in previous or subsequent normal pregnancies.

In the absence of definite medical knowledge about the causes of most miscarriages, the process of finding a personally satisfying explanation seems eminently reasonable, if not actually necessary. One key motive is clearly the avoidance of the same fate in the next pregnancy: 'I wish I knew [the cause], then I wouldn't have to worry about the next time', as one woman put it. Or, as another said, in answer to our question about what caused the miscarriage, 'If I knew that, I would be having another pregnancy!' It's also interesting that over time the factors blamed for miscarriage may change. Tracey Hurst:

I have a very busy job which, although I enjoy, is at times very stressful, and I normally work about 45–50 hours per week plus two and a half hours per day travelling. The week before the miscarriage I worked extra to the above hours, and although my GP said this wasn't the cause I did for a short time blame overwork for the miscarriage. Also during the latter couple of weeks of the pregnancy I was worried (unnecessarily) about my husband's business. I now blame nothing for the miscarriage, but perhaps would be a little anxious in a future pregnancy in case I experienced another miscarriage, and would probably feel guilty if I didn't leave work straightaway. My husband is still 'looking for something to blame'. He thinks my job probably caused it and is anxious for me to leave my particular job before I start another pregnancy.

Or, as another mother wrote:

> I have to convince myself it was some deformity in the growth of the fetus, although I have in the past blamed it on any number of things, e.g., drinking, dieting before conception, allowing myself to get tired, lifting a heavy weight in the first weeks, etc. etc.

An essential feature of the 'why me?' syndrome is the tendency to blame yourself as the cause of the miscarriage. In a way it seems obvious that if your body hasn't been able to hold onto the fetus for long enough to transform it into a live baby, then there must be some error in your behaviour or, at the very least, something wrong with your mental attitudes during pregnancy. Perhaps, as Dorothy Alexander wondered, that particular fetus hadn't been wanted or loved enough? Or, as Tracey Hurst saw it, her work (which to add insult to injury she actually enjoyed) must have been counter to her fetus's welfare. Husbands, it has to be said, are not immune from the 'why me?' syndrome. Abigail Murray thought her miscarriage 'was something to do with the fact that I had been unwell and hadn't eaten properly for about two weeks' but her husband 'thought it might be because a "dud" sperm fertilized my egg and my body rejected it.'

This tendency for women (and men) to blame their own behaviour for causing miscarriage very rarely, of course, has any basis in fact. This is probably why enjoyable experiences thought capable of damaging pregnancy are typically a focus of greater self-blame than those which weren't enjoyed. Holidays, sex, overindulgence in food and a job one really likes are examples of factors that appear to occasion extra guilt. This attitude is, of course, hardly rational, and is some kind of heritage of the puritan religious ethic that personal misfortune is always caused by personal wrong-doing, and God metes out a punishment for every sacrilegious pleasure.

We referred in our introduction to a survey of miscarriage done by a physician called Granville in London in 1819. We have compared what the women in Granville's survey thought had caused their miscarriages with the answers given by the women in our survey carried out 164 years later and shown in table 5.1. Some of the 'causes' that existed in 1983 did not exist in 1819 – for instance the pill, the coil, and terms such as 'incompetent cervix', 'placental insufficiency' and 'blighted ovum'. Allowing for this, we have tried to make Granville's categories as comparable as possible to those in table 5.1 (page 114).

Table 5.2 **The causes of miscarriage mentioned by women in 1819**

	% women mentioning
Abnormal fetus	3
Illness/accidents/medication in pregnancy	35
Overdoing it	9
Shock, worry, etc.	28
Local uterine problems*	19
'Improper physical and moral treatment of pregnant women'	3
Don't know	3
Total	100

* 'local or general fulness' [sic];
  'excessive irritability of the womb':
  'increased local action'

Source: Granville, 1819

Women in 1819 appear to have been more certain about the causes of their miscarriages than women in 1983 – only 3 per cent didn't know, as against 23 per cent in 1983. Moreover, few of them (also only 3 per cent) thought the cause of the miscarriage was an abnormal fetus. By far the largest group of causes – mentioned by 35 per cent of the women – were illness, local or general debility, falls, blows and incautious use of medicines. The large proportion (28 per cent) of Granville's sample who thought miscarriage due to emotional factors such as shock or worry is also noteworthy. The proportions naming 'overdoing it' as the culprit are remarkably similar (9 per cent in 1819, 11 per cent in 1983), and as to what was meant by the penultimate category in table 5.2, 'improper physical and moral treatment of pregnant women', Granville is delightfully vague, leaving the answers to be supplied by his readers' imaginations!

Cultural attitudes to miscarriage

Given the prevailing state of maternal health in the early years of the nineteenth century, the women in Granville's sample were probably right in believing illness and debility to be a principal cause of miscarriage. We do not know what the incidence of miscarriage has been in different societies at different stages in history, but we do know that attitudes towards childbirth, motherhood, women, miscarriage and death in general have changed profoundly. It would not be too far-fetched to say that modern attitudes towards these topics is probably making adjustment to the experience of miscarriage more difficult for women today than for their sisters in the past.

Throughout most of history and in most of the world's cultures, women's main preoccupation has been to prevent too many births. In colonial America, for example, average family size was eight children – the average married woman had eight livebirths, although functioning family size was nearer five, because many children died; and the miscarriage rate was almost certainly high as well. Most women used various strategies to limit the number of children in their families – from encouraging their husbands to use coitus interruptus, to diligent douching, from use of sponges and drugs in the vagina, to deliberate abortion and even infanticide. Medical histories of contraception are replete with the most imaginative and and unpleasant ways to avoid conception and bring about abortion, which testify to the enormous responsibility women throughout history have shouldered in attempting to bring into the world only those children whom they could reasonably hope to look after well. Induced abortion, that is, abortion induced by women themselves, was part of this responsible attitude to motherhood, although, of course, frowned on by the Church and also often by the State interested in securing a birth-rate adequate to replace the population.

Under conditions in which fertility was difficult to control and in which birth and death rates were high, women's attitudes to both induced and spontaneous abortion may well have been different. There is evidence to suggest that induced abortion was accepted and discussed by women as a necessary part of female existence, and miscarriage may well, in these circumstances, have tended to be viewed in a more positive light. In *Dear Dr Stopes* there is a letter written in the 1920s by a Sheffield woman to Dr Marie Stopes, pioneer of birth control in Britain:

Well, Dr, I have had five children in five years, two are dead for which I thank God for, the three I have are always ailing, they seem bloodless . . . I and my three children have to live and sleep in one small room, my last baby was born three months ago, it was night time and while I was been seen my husband had to sit on the doorstep in the rain . . .

and another wrote:

This last two months or rather two monthly periods I have had two shocks. The first time after being overdue a week I took, at intervals, nineteen female pills and a bottle of medicine before I became poorly. Almost the same thing happened during my last period, I was thirteen days overdue . . . My husband swears he will kill himself rather than see me suffer with child again, and I myself would prefer death first . . .

It's easy to see that in these circumstances women who had at least some surviving children would rather suffer miscarriage than childbirth. Another consideration was the greater danger of dying in childbirth – around forty times greater than the risk today. (And without modern methods of pain relief the pain of childbirth may have been a factor in some women's minds.) However, to say that miscarriage may have been a generally less traumatic experience in the eighteenth, nineteenth or early twentieth centuries must in the end be a matter of conjecture. Was a lesser value attached to children because infant death rates were epidemic? We really don't know. There are few surviving documents which give us attitudes rather than merely statistics. One such is *Maternity: Letters from Working Women*, a collection of 160 letters collected by the Women's Cooperative Guild and published in Britain in 1915. The published 160 letters were a sub-sample of 386 returned in response to a short questionnaire sent out by the Guild to provide ammunition for a campaign to improve the level of maternity and child health care. Out of the 348 women who had children and gave the necessary information, 42 per cent reported stillbirths or miscarriages. Among these women the average number of miscarriages was two, but the sample included two unfortunate women who had ten miscarriages each and five who had between six and eight. One woman who had two children and three miscarriages wrote of her experiences:

After my first little one I went out too soon, with the result that I got a cold in the ovaries, which caused me the most acute pain, and for quite a month every few steps I walked I would sit down. I have had several miscarriages – one caused through carelessness in jumping up to take some clothes off the line when it commenced to rain, instead of getting a chair to stand on, another through taking some pills which were delivered as samples to the door, and a third through a fright by a cow whilst on holidays. So you will see I realize to the full the care and thought a woman requires. I may say that to me the after-effects of the miscarriages have been worse than confinements, for it takes months to get over the weakness.

This letter was written about the time that free medical care for pregnant women began to get off the ground in Britain. Over the period since then there have been enormous changes affecting the health of mothers and children and reflected in greatly decreased death rates of mothers in pregnancy and during and following childbirth, and of babies in late pregnancy and throughout infancy. Fertility rates have also fallen, so that average family size is now 2.4 children. Add to that the securing of legal termination of pregnancy with the 1967 Abortion Act, and the use of more effective contraceptive methods, particularly the pill, and you have a context for miscarriage which is quite different from the one that existed when the letters in *Maternity* were written.

Many young women growing up today expect to have only successful pregnancies. They assume that if they decide to have a baby they will be able to conceive, and that once pregnancy has started it will continue until the birth of a healthy baby. Miscarriage is one of the events that challenges this set of assumptions. Others are infertility, stillbirth, perinatal death, and the birth and survival of handicapped children. All these tragedies (except perhaps infertility) are rarer than they used to be, but the fact that they still happen must draw our attention to the limits of modern medicine and our technological society. It is most unlikely that the loss or imperfection of some pregnancies and some children will ever be entirely preventable. Almost an equal tragedy is the conspiracy of silence (or denial) that we seem to have drawn over this negative side of parenthood.

As we have shown in this book, miscarriage is a common occurrence, indeed it may be a more common occurrence than childbirth. Yet in lots of ways our society doesn't acknowledge this. In both their formal and informal education children are prepared only for the straightforward versions of reproduction and family life, whereas perhaps it would be fairer to indicate the kinds of difficulties that do occur and how they can be coped with. (We are thinking here not only of events such as miscarriage, but also of occurrences like unemployment.) Because they are not widely discussed, normal 'deviations' such as miscarriage are even more of a shock when they do happen.

This is one of the most important ways in which cultural attitudes towards miscarriage affect women's individual experiences, and it is tied up with attitudes towards death in general. Birth, death and illness have, in the twentieth century, been 'medicalized', that is, turned into medical events managed by doctors in institutions called hospitals. They have lost their character as an integral part of community life for which the community as a whole takes responsibility. Yet individuals still need to mourn, and the mourning is more difficult once the social character has been removed from birth and death. As a society we lack the accepted rituals for mourning which we used to have – and many societies still have – not only for the deaths of adults but for pregnancy loss as well. Anthropologists studying non-industrialized small-scale societies often note elaborate mourning rituals which help the individual through a process of adjustment following the deaths of relatives and friends. For example, the Siriono people of South America consider the miscarried fetus human enough to need ritual mourning. Both parents mourn for three days, scarring their legs and adorning their hair with feathers. We don't necessarily recommend these procedures (!) but note with interest that among the Siriono the rituals used for mourning miscarried fetuses are exactly the same as those used for any dead person.

Mourning after miscarriage

Many women in our survey recognized their need to go through a period of mourning following a miscarriage. Some women will mourn without realizing they're doing it, and for some there may be less of a need to mourn – all these reactions are quite normal. Over the last few years it has been increasingly realized that parents who have a stillborn baby or one who dies shortly after birth may need help to acknowledge and work through their grief, and that the inclination of many hospital staff to dispose of the baby's body and cheer the parents up with clichés about being young enough to have another is not at all helpful. Yet it appears that the new insight into the emotional realities of stillbirth and perinatal death have not yet been applied to pregnancy losses:

Although you have lost a baby, like a woman who has a stillbirth, you are not allowed the same feelings of grief or bereavement. The doctors are eager to scrape you clean physically, but do not seem interested in your mental well-being.

Miscarriage doesn't seem to carry the same kind of consideration and sympathy as a stillbirth or a child's death. But the sense of loss is still there, even in those early weeks.

Mourning a miscarried fetus may be easier if the fetus has been seen by the mother and is therefore more tangible as the person who is being mourned:

I think the worst thing about it for me was the fact that your grief is 'intangible' – no name for the baby, never seeing it, no grave to put a flower on, just the horrible thought of it being slung in an incinerator or worse, when you had wanted it so much.

Many women spoke of having 'lost part of myself'. Apart from being literally true, there is also the sense in which the lost fetus is what could have transformed the woman into a mother, and the miscarriage has thus removed (albeit perhaps only temporarily) the woman's identification with the mother role. One woman talked about feeling 'alone in a world of mothers': this put it well. Another common phrase used was feeling 'empty inside' – perhaps more likely if the miscarriage is a late one, but a description that also serves to make the metaphorical point about the emotional numbness, which may be the most immediate reaction to a miscarriage.

Several women describe feeling rather elated, 'high', just after the miscarriage. Thus Angela Parkinson, who had a D & C following an incomplete abortion at thirteen weeks – her second miscarriage – says:

In the week following the miscarriage I felt rather 'high'. It did not hit me that I was no longer expecting a baby. I was also relieved to have survived the event. I was the centre of attention and still in a state of shock. Then, suddenly, and apparently to do with the drop of certain hormone levels, progesterone in particular, I experienced a severe bout of weeping. The realization of what had happened hit me very hard. People no longer asked how I was or tried to console me. I was expected to resume life as it had been before being pregnant. But I felt disorientated. I felt as if I had lost part of myself. It became difficult to cry, but I needed to grieve for those lost babies almost as if they had been born and then died.

I believe that the most important element in recovering from a miscarriage is to let the grief out in some way. I say recover – but I don't believe many women ever completely recover. They merely learn to live with their regret and in time accept their loss.

This reaction of temporary elation has also been described in patients after surgery. It seems, as Angela acknowledges, to have something to do with relief at personal survival. In the case of miscarriage, the depression which may follow can go on for many months, or lift and descend again:

I suffered from delayed shock in the form of depression and anxiety some six months after my actual miscarriage. It felt like a physical reaction too – all the more galling because I thought that I had got 'over it' quite well.

The occasion of the baby's would-be birth date was mentioned by many women as reawakening the feeling of unassuaged grief:

The biggest adjustment has been thinking of April as a normal month rather than the baby's EDD [expected date of delivery] . . .

I also had a bad time when my babies were due to be born and I'd thought I was coping well . . . It didn't help me when in November [the baby's EDD] a midwife arrived at my door to see the baby. The hospital hadn't informed the district nurses of the miscarriage, so it was very upsetting for myself and the poor nurse.

As one woman said, even after the would-be birth date has passed, 'you keep thinking of what he/she would be doing as the months and years go by'; and as another woman who was unable to have children after recurrent miscarriages said: 'we are low just now because had our first child been born, she would be eleven this week, which means she would be commencing secondary education next term'.

Sometimes post-miscarriage reactions are not easily classifiable by the mother as depression. Acknowledgement of grief may be blocked by the necessity of resuming 'normal' life again (how life can ever be normal again is a question asked by many women). Having another child or children to care for may in this sense be a mixed blessing as Tessa Moore found:

When I came home from hospital I hoped I wouldn't see anyone and dreaded the phone ringing for me. I copied out page after page of recipes. I felt very numb and blank, but I cried a lot and had to spend a lot of time alone. I couldn't tolerate too much noise or activity. I was physically exhausted and slightly anaemic. Apart from an appointment, weeks away, I had no further contact with the medical profession. I felt stranded. I didn't know what to do with my time – when I had been pregnant, even when sunbathing, I had felt busy, now I seemed to have nothing to do.

I appeared calm and talked about normal things, but I was really very far away. As I was unable to immediately verbalize my feelings – they were too basic and hadn't surfaced as words – people took me at face value. I know there were people who said, 'Oh Tessa's not the sort to get too upset, she's sensible.' The thing was I dared not let myself go beyond the tears that I couldn't help, because I was frightened of the pain I would have to acknowledge. It took time to be able to do that. I also had to look after a two-year-old child and do the shopping, so the natural unfoldings of my feelings were further suppressed and had to be 'fitted in' between domestic obligations.

I remember that for the first month or two my mind seemed to be racing – it was like being on an express train which wouldn't stop. I developed an anxiety about my son falling out of an upstairs window. I sat around a lot and did nothing. I couldn't face large social gatherings. Outwardly I appeared quite normal, I had to keep one part of me behaving as it was used to doing. I felt and still feel, very confused and terribly, at times overwhelmingly, empty.

In most of the accounts of miscarriage we received, it is clear that the major physical and emotional impact is on mothers not fathers. Nevertheless, just as birth and parenthood are increasingly shared experiences for many couples, so for some of the women in our survey miscarriage was an experience undergone with their partners, at least in an emotional sense. We saw in chapter 4 the important supportive role played by many husbands; miscarriage may thus be an event that brings the couple closer together, uniting them in their grief. But it may also have a divisive effect, and especially if a woman feels her partner doesn't understand her reactions (or vice versa) there can be a strain on the relationship. Perhaps he doesn't appreciate the extent to which she feels she has lost a child – or the depth of her fears that she will never achieve motherhood? Or perhaps he withdraws into himself, finds it difficult to put any words to his feelings, thereby creating the quite false impression that he *has* no feelings. This kind of response was described by several women:

My husband was revising for exams when the miscarriage happened and so was not able to give me any comfort until later on. I think this too is very important as the baby belongs to you both – I also felt that he didn't seem very upset and felt a little disappointed at the time, although I realized he was very busy.

And one later revised her opinion:

I can remember, at the time, I accused my husband of not caring. He didn't break down in tears all the time after I came home from hospital as I did and he didn't constantly want to talk about what might have been. It was only much later (and even more so after the birth of our son) that I realized the awful strain he had been under. It was just as much his concern, but he had to carry on working and, more importantly, he had to be able to offer me terrific strength. If he had openly showed all his feelings we would both have floundered for months.

The same response was described by Dorothy Alexander

earlier in this chapter; she spoke of her husband 'saving his own sadness' until she was pregnant and happy again.

Sexual intercourse may temporarily become a problem after miscarriage, because of ambivalent attitudes towards the prospect of a future pregnancy, or because the woman's sense of her own sexuality has been disturbed by her body's failure to produce a healthy child. All these reactions are better discussed than hidden, though both partners may be better accepting that their best confidantes could at least for a while be other people, especially close friends who have had similar experiences.

However difficult the experience of miscarriage may be, it is at least a curable illness for the mother: it is something from which she will eventually recover – even though, as we have seen, she is not likely to forget what has happened. One woman said:

> When I went into hospital a patient was dying from cancer. When I listened to that lady, I thought I was lucky that I had something I would recover from. Even before my operation and D & C, I was planning ahead to the time I would get pregnant again.

The physical aftermath

Finally in this chapter we discuss some of the practical questions that may concern women after a miscarriage. These are often not seen to be strictly medical, but they may actually be very important at the time. Both from our personal experiences and from the replies to our questionnaires, we have tried to predict what these questions will be and to give some practical guidelines in our answers.

1. Do I have to stay in bed after a miscarriage?
Only as long as you feel tired and want to.

2. When will the bleeding stop after a miscarriage (or D & C)?

The length of time that bleeding continues and the amount is very variable, as is the colour. It may be bright red, pink or brown, with or without clots. Normally it has stopped by two or three weeks after the miscarriage. If the bleeding persists after this, or if at any time it gets very smelly (a possible indication of an infection), or it is very heavy with a large number of large clots, it is important to contact your doctor as some bits of the placenta may still be left in the womb and will need to be removed.

3. When can I use tampons?

It is not a good idea to use tampons while bleeding during and following a miscarriage, because the cervix (neck of the womb) will still be open and the whole womb is especially sensitive to infection – it is rather like an open wound. Tampons in the vagina are thought to be more likely to introduce infection, so it is probably best to use sanitary towels for the bleeding during and immediately after a miscarriage, but it is all right to use tampons during the next period.

4. When can I have a bath?

Immediately. Some people recommend showers as preferable, but there appears to be no risk of infection or any other problems when having baths straightaway. In fact, many women find baths a great source of comfort. Douching is not a good idea.

5. Will I get milk in my breasts?

The later on in pregnancy you have a miscarriage, the more likely it is that you will get milk in your breasts. Of women who miscarry at nineteen weeks, 80–90 per cent will secrete milk, whereas the figure is 5–10 per cent for women miscarrying at twelve weeks. If you do get milk coming in, your breasts will feel full and tender and sometimes lumpy, and may leak milk. This can last anywhere from a couple of days to a week or longer.

Most doctors do not recommend drug treatment to deal with the problem of milk secretion after miscarriage, as it usually settles down alone. Some doctors occasionally use oestrogens or a drug called bromocriptine, but both drugs can have unpleasant side effects. If you are very worried by milk secretion, it's worth discussing the problem with your doctor.

6. *When can I go back to work?*
The decision to go back to work is really entirely up to you. Ideally, you should go back to work when you feel fit enough – for most women this is within a week; however, if there have been complications it may take longer. If you have had an anaesthetic for a D & C you are unlikely to feel fit enough for work immediately.

Having a miscarriage need not necessarily stop you from working – so that if your work is vital to you (for financial or other reasons), it would be OK to go back to work within a day or two.

7. *When is it all right to resume intercourse?*
The general consensus is as soon as the bleeding stops. The reason given for not having intercourse before this is the risk of infection, but this claim may not be true and perhaps when you feel like it should be the answer. You may not feel like having intercourse for some time after the bleeding stops, and the feelings of both partners on this need to be respected. After having a baby, many women feel a decreased sexual drive which may last for some months. This may also occur after a miscarriage.

8. *When do I need to start using contraception following a miscarriage?*
You can ovulate at any time after a miscarriage, so if you are going to have intercourse very soon after a miscarriage and do not want to conceive instantly (see section on pregnancy spacing) you need to use some form of birth control. You can start the pill on the day after a miscarriage and you are then

safe after fourteen days, or you can wait till the next period and start taking it as usual. If you use a diaphragm it is a good idea to have the size checked as soon as you want to start using it after a miscarriage. If you want to use a coil (or IUCD) as contraception it is best to wait for six weeks after the miscarriage before having it fitted because the uterus is still rather soft, and there is a slightly increased risk of perforation at the time of insertion. You would therefore need to use another method of contraception until the coil can be fitted. If you have any queries it is worth discussing contraception with your GP or Family Planning doctor.

9. *How long should I wait before getting pregnant again?*

It is difficult to give very definite advice here. It is known from animal experiments that conceptions occurring very shortly after a previous pregnancy are more likely to fail (either they are absorbed or do not proceed normally). Whether the same mechanism works in humans is not known. Looking at data on pregnancy spacing and perinatal mortality (deaths of babies from 28 weeks of pregnancy to the end of the first week of life), it appears that a short gap between pregnancies (six months or less) is more likely to be associated with a slight risk to the baby in the next pregnancy. However, the explanation is probably that those women who for other reasons run higher risks than average of having unsuccessful pregnancies tend to have smaller gaps between pregnancies in order to 'compensate' for a previous miscarriage or perinatal death.

The statistical picture is complicated, and we can really only conclude that it is not known whether it is a bad idea to get pregnant again very quickly after a miscarriage. As we see in chapter 8, many doctors recommend waiting three months before trying to conceive again, though the ones we spoke to based this advice on clinical impression rather than hard statistics, because as yet there are none. Thus, how long you wait before trying to conceive again depends on many different factors including, for example, how old you are (if you are over forty you will probably want to try again as soon as possible because the number of years during which you can conceive is more limited). There is a psychological as well as a physical consideration here in that some couples need a period of grieving before feeling ready to embark upon another pregnancy. This certainly seems to be so following a stillbirth or the death of a baby soon after it is born, where it has been shown that psychological problems are more likely to occur if the parents attempt to have a 'replacement' child straight away. Until we have more information, waiting for three months seems a reasonable compromise at a physical level, but at a psychological level it may need to be longer.

6 Ectopic Pregnancy

After a year of trying to conceive, I referred myself to a fertility clinic and eventually discovered that my fallopian tubes were blocked, due to an infection associated with an IUCD infection. Two years later, at the age of thirty-one, I had tubal surgery to attempt to rectify the problem, and a month after the operation I discovered that I was, indeed, pregnant. I was on the verge of writing to the doctor who had performed the deed to congratulate him on his success when I began experiencing the most excruciating stomach cramps. A visit to casualty established that the pregnancy was ectopic and at eleven weeks my right tube was removed. (Susan Wheeler)

An ectopic pregnancy is, literally, a pregnancy that is 'out-of-place' (from the Greek *ektopos*). We have decided to devote a short chapter to ectopic pregnancy, not because it is an especially common form of miscarriage (in fact it's quite rare), but because it can be difficult to diagnose, and it is important for women to be familiar with the likely symptoms, so that they can get medical help when it's needed.

Since the normal place for a fetus to grow is inside the womb, an ectopic pregnancy is one that embeds outside the normal intrauterine location. Most ectopic pregnancies develop in one of the fallopian tubes. In one series of 150 patients with ectopic pregnancies studied in America, 90.6 per cent were tubal; the rest were either found to be cornual (where the fallopian tube joins the uterus), ovarian or in the abdominal cavity (see figure 6.1; table 6.1). The right and left tubes are about equally involved in ectopic pregnancy.

Figure 6.1 **Possible sites of ectopic pregnancy**

 Abdominal

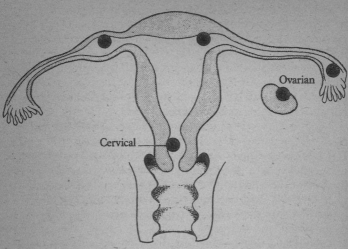

Ovarian

Cervical

Table 6.1 **Site of implantation in American study**

	%
Tubal	90.6
Abdominal	2.7
Cornual	2.7
Ovarian	2.7
Unspecified/combined	1.4
Total	100.0

Source: Hlavin *et al.*, 1978

Incidence and causes

Ectopic pregnancy was first described in AD 936 and first operated on successfully in 1759. But although it's been a recognized hazard of conception for a long time, remarkably little is known either about its true incidence (as a proportion of all pregnancies) or about what causes it.

One estimate is that on average one in every 200 conceptions is ectopic (this figure is for England and Wales in 1976). The risk of an ectopic pregnancy rises with age. Although the risk of dying from an ectopic pregnancy is much lower than it used to be, deaths from this cause have become much more important in overall maternal mortality (deaths due to, or associated with, childbearing) as other causes (for example deaths due to infection during or after childbirth) have become much less frequent.

The two factors that have been discussed most as possible causes of ectopic pregnancy are infection and use of an IUCD. The argument is that if a woman has had an infection of the fallopian tubes then an ectopic pregnancy is more likely, because infection has damaged the normal function of the tube, which is to conduct the fertilized ovum safely to the body of the uterus. This is one reason why ectopic pregnancy is more likely following a history of infertility. Similarly, an IUCD is thought to interfere with intrauterine implantation and thus to increase the risk of implantation elsewhere. It does seem to be true that pregnancies in users of IUCDs are more likely to be ectopic – about six times more likely than in the general population. Of course insertion of an IUCD may activate an infection or be itself more likely in women with a history of infection – which all means that the causal association must be regarded as strictly non-proven. Other theories have also been advanced as to the causes of ectopic pregnancy: these include previous induced abortion, use of progestogen-only contraceptive pills, and accidental migration of the ovum from one side of the pelvis to the other (resulting in a pregnancy which is ready to implant before it reaches the uterus). We really have no evidence at the moment on which to judge the accuracy of these theories.

There is, however, no doubt that ectopic pregnancy is on the increase. There has been a rise from 3.2 per 1000 estimated conceptions in England and Wales in 1966 to 5.0 in 1976. An increased incidence has also been reported in other countries – including Finland, Sweden, Czechoslovakia and the United States.

Symptoms and diagnosis

Susan Wheeler, quoted at the head of this chapter, experienced pain as the first symptom of her ectopic pregnancy. Table 6.2 is taken from the American study referred to above, and shows the actual frequency of various symptoms experienced by women with ectopic pregnancies in that study.

Table 6.2 **Symptoms experienced by 150 women with ectopic pregnancies**

Symptom	*% women experiencing*
Pain	96
Vaginal bleeding	75
Missed period(s)	63
Nausea	20
Vomiting	15
Fainting	13
Dizziness	9
Weakness	9
Passage of tissue	5
Breast engorgement	3
Fever and chills	3
Diarrhoea	3
Abdominal fullness	1
Shoulder pain	1
Frequent urination	1

Source: Hlavin *et al.*, 1978

Pain and bleeding are the most common symptoms: nearly two-thirds of the women, in addition, missed one or more periods. These symptoms are also characteristic of threatened miscarriage in normally placed pregnancies, and, just to confuse matters further, the pain may be mistaken for other surgical emergencies such as appendicitis. Ectopic pregnancy can therefore be hard to diagnose, as Alex Cartwright found out:

I am recovering from an ectopic pregnancy which was wrongly diagnosed as appendicitis. After one day in hospital, I went home, still with pain. A week later, my doctor suggested I had a D and C done and I went into hospital for two days under observation. I had been in great pain, and wasn't allowed painkillers because my urine specimens were all positive. My [ultrasound] scan was negative (by that I mean nothing showed up), but I was discharged by a registrar who told me he didn't believe in scans and to take life easy and to return to work.

Alex's pain and bleeding didn't stop and her GP prescribed bedrest, on the grounds that she was probably miscarrying. Eventually she visited the hospital antenatal clinic where 'a doctor became interested in my shoulder pain and diagnosed a possible ectopic pregnancy'. A further ultrasound scan confirmed the likelihood of this and Alex went on to have surgery: one of her fallopian tubes and one ovary were removed.

In a tubal pregnancy – the most frequent form of ectopic pregnancy – the fertilized egg implants in the fallopian tube. As it does so, many of the changes characteristic of early normal pregnancy take place: HCG (the 'pregnancy hormone') is produced, the womb enlarges slightly and the woman's next period is suppressed or delayed, the breasts become tender, and a urine pregnancy test may be positive. About half of all ectopic pregnancies are positive on such a test, and about half are negative. A newer test, known as a radioimmunoassay test, is a more sensitive detector of pregnancy hormone levels and may even be able to distinguish ruptured from unruptured ectopic pregnancies.

After some time, however, the tube with its enlarging pregnancy will stretch and eventually burst. This happens most often between the eighth and twelfth week – and in about 35 per cent of all cases of ectopic pregnancy. This will cause pain and bleeding which is occasionally very acute and dramatic: the woman may collapse because of the pain and sudden internal haemorrhage. But more often the tubal rupture is gradual and the symptoms are chronic – vaginal bleeding that stops and starts, pain that may or may not be located on one or other side of the lower abdomen. Particularly for women who have not had a 'normal' miscarriage before, these symptoms may not suggest a misplaced pregnancy. When the tube ruptures it is normal for the embryo to die and be reabsorbed by the mother's body. This sounds eerie, but is normal among mammals (and happens, too, in some fated intrauterine pregnancies). Whether or not positive results continue to be produced on hormonal pregnancy tests varies, but usually the symptoms subside and the tests become negative.

As we saw from Alex Cartwright's description of her ectopic pregnancy, it is hard to diagnose an early unruptured ectopic pregnancy. At this stage, as we have said, pregnancy tests are not a great deal of help. An ultrasound scan can show whether or not there is a gestation sac *inside* the uterus (it can show this by about six weeks from the start of the last normal period) – but even with ultrasound it can be difficult to know what is happening *outside* the uterus, if that's where the pregnancy is. Abdominal and pelvic examination by a doctor or midwife can give important clues, but often it is impossible to distinguish an ectopic from a normal pregnancy by examination alone. Blood tests can show whether or not internal bleeding has started, but even then the bodies of normal healthy women may quickly make up for the effects of blood loss, so that these tests are not very helpful either. The shoulder pain described by Alex Cartwright does, however, point especially to an ectopic pregnancy. The pain is what is called 'referred pain' – the site of the problem is not the shoulder but the pain is felt here because of the pressure of internal bleeding in the abdominal cavity.

Only 1 per cent of women with ectopic pregnancies report shoulder pain (table 6.2) so that still leaves 99 per cent to be diagnosed. Overall, as an editorial in the *British Medical Journal* put it, for the doctor 'the best way to diagnose an ectopic pregnancy is to think of it'. Similarly, by being aware of the possibility, and sensitive to the way their bodies are behaving, women who have ectopic pregnancies can help themselves by drawing the doctor's attention to this fact early on. It is very important to get access to medical treatment if you have an ectopic pregnancy, because this is a condition that can be fatal to the mother. A few women in Britain still die every year from ectopic pregnancy which has not been diagnosed or treated in time.

Treatment

Only very rarely in ectopic pregnancy does the baby survive. In such case the delivery is by abdominal surgery. The most frequent train of events is either for an emergency operation if internal bleeding is very sudden or severe, or for the doctor's suspicions to be aroused to the point where it is decided to operate and see what's going on. A laparoscopy may be done first: this involves viewing the pelvis with an instrument inserted through an inch-wide slit in the navel. The way to remove a tubal pregnancy is by an incision in the lower abdomen (laparotomy). Occasionally, if the pregnancy is very early, the whole thing may be gently 'milked out' of the tube and the tube thus preserved. But more commonly, and certainly in cases of tubal rupture, a salpingectomy (removal of the tube) is done. Sometimes, as in Alex Cartwright's case, the ovary on that side is also removed (salpingo-oophorectomy). This is done either because the site of the ectopic pregnancy is the ovary, or because the ovary is damaged in some way, or because the gynaecologist believes that future fertility will be improved if it is removed along with the tube. One theory is that if you remove the ovary on the tubeless side in order to improve fertility, then ovulation will in future be confined to the ovary with a tube next to it ('putting all your eggs into one basket'). There is no evidence that taking out the ovary as well increases the chance of subsequent normal pregnancy, and the procedure has the disadvantage that what is removed is a healthy ovary – it's not generally a good idea to remove healthy organs!

Surgery for an ectopic pregnancy is always done under general anaesthesia. The physical after-effects are the same as for any other major gynaecological surgery – a certain amount of pain from the operation wound, sleepiness and tiredness from the anaesthetic. If there has been a lot of bleeding, the woman will be given a blood transfusion. The stay in hospital is generally 5–10 days. The incision may be either vertical (down the abdomen below the navel) or horizontal (just below the pubic hair line). Wherever it is, the scar may look horrific at first, but when the stitches are taken out it will fade to a pale silvery line and will eventually be scarcely noticeable. The scar is not a problem in a subsequent normal pregnancy because it is not on the uterus itself.

As with normal miscarriages the end of an ectopic pregnancy will be followed by some vaginal bleeding, as the uterus relieves itself of the impact of a pregnancy. After the first few days, it is probably quite all right to use tampons. Intercourse can begin again as soon as you feel physically and emotionally ready – but remember that you have had major surgery, and there may be pain under pressure at the site of the operation for some time. Your menstrual cycle should not be affected by removal of a tube, or by removal of one ovary, and normal periods usually return within a few weeks.

Future fertility

The chances of a successful full-term pregnancy after an ectopic pregnancy are generally somewhat lowered, but much depends on the cause of the misplaced pregnancy (see below), and on each woman's gynaecological history. The overall risk of a second ectopic is about 10 per cent (which compares with a risk of 0.4 per cent in women who have not already had an ectopic pregnancy). Even women who have two ectopic pregnancies may still have a chance of having a successful pregnancy, assuming of course that they still have all (or most of) one fallopian tube. This means that if you've had one ectopic pregnancy you have a 90 per cent chance of an intrauterine pregnancy if you become pregnant again. The fact of having had an ectopic pregnancy does not in itself necessarily prejudice the success of the next pregnancy once you get pregnant and the pregnancy is in the right place.

Reactions to ectopic pregnancy

Susan Wheeler went on to say that after her ectopic pregnancy she was told that her chances of a normal conception were 'quite high'.

'But I also know', she said, 'that having had one ectopic pregnancy my chances of having another are increased . . . I agonize frequently about what to do. Emotionally, I don't feel able to cope with another ectopic pregnancy, I still haven't got over the last . . . I have given myself another three years in which to decide, years which will undoubtedly be fraught with periods of extreme depression and mixed feelings every time one of my contemporaries gives birth.'

An ectopic pregnancy can be followed with all the usual

reactions of grief, anger, confusion and so on that attend a normal miscarriage. But in addition there are three problems specific to ectopic pregnancy. The first is the inaccessibility of the fetus to the woman who lost it: in most cases, since it briefly lived and died and never emerged from her body, it is difficult to believe it was really there. Some women may find this helps them to recover but others may find it difficult.

The second problem peculiar to ectopic pregnancy is the task of adjusting to the surgery that resulted. There is the scar, which may at first look awful and be a cause of depression (somewhat like the scar of a caesarean section). But there is also the loss of a fallopian tube and maybe an ovary as well. These organs, like the womb itself, are part of one's life as a woman and most women do not part with them lightly. There may well be a feeling of mutilation, and anxiety that one is not a 'proper' woman any longer. Such thoughts usually become less dominant with time, but they can have quite an obsessional character about them for a while.

The third difficulty is the one referred to by Susan Wheeler – to get pregnant again, or not? This seems like altogether a more weighty decision when there is the prospect of another ectopic pregnancy on the horizon which might finish one's chances of ever having a baby. In the end the decision can only be made on an individual basis. It is worth remembering that the whole of life is a risk, and a risk that *isn't* taken may be just as much regretted as one that is:

My two children were six and seven when I decided to get pregnant again. I had always wanted a third child but there had never seemed to be a convenient time to get pregnant – now there was.

I conceived the first month we didn't use contraception. I was almost sure I was pregnant, but then I had a short and light period which was a few days late. My breasts maintained their usual pre-menstrual (pregnant?) state and I eventually went to a chemist for a pregnancy test. He said it was 'just below positive'. Then followed a long saga of tests, hospital admissions etc., culminating in the diagnosis of an already-ruptured tubal pregnancy eleven weeks after my last normal period.

I was absolutely shattered – I wasn't the kind of person to have that sort of problem, was I? Why had it happened? Why hadn't it been diagnosed sooner? I hadn't even got half way through these reactions when I conceived again, this time accidentally while using my cap. This was the only unplanned pregnancy I had ever had. It was not ectopic – but in the right place, briefly, for that pregnancy ended in an ordinary miscarriage at twelve weeks. Again I had no idea why it had happened. Three months later another conception – intended, intrauterine, and successful: an eight-and-a-half pound baby ten months later. No one knows why that one worked, either!'

7 Treatment

The ideal outcome of pregnancy is that it should end with the birth of a normal baby at between 38 and 42 weeks after conception. Miscarriage obviously falls short of this ideal, but, as we have stressed, miscarriage is often nature's way of getting rid of a fetus that is in some way abnormal. However, there are many normal fetuses who also miscarry, and it is for these pregnancies that parents and doctors alike want safe and effective treatment.

The development of safe and effective means to prevent the recurrent miscarriage of normally formed fetuses would thus undoubtedly be a major achievement. Many attempts have been made to find treatments which appear to have a scientific basis for their action and seem likely to be safe. Over the years many claims have been made for different therapies, and because doctors feel so anxious to do something and women very much want something done to help them, the result has been the giving of treatments and advice which have not always been shown to work. (This, of course, also applies to many other areas of medicine.) Sometimes the psychological help given by having *something* suggested or done may be treatment in itself – but if this is so, it is important to establish that the 'something' does not have any serious adverse effects or problems. It is equally important that doctors should not be blamed for *not* doing things when in fact inaction may be the most appropriate course, because there is actually no treatment to offer. It is also very important to remember that for doctors, nurses and patients alike, discussion and explanation in themselves represent a huge part of the management of any disease.

Having said this, what we will go on to do in this chapter is to review the most commonly used physical treatments for miscarriage, looking closely both at their effectiveness in preventing miscarriage and at their safety. Even if a treatment has not been shown to be effective, as long as it is considered harmless doctors and patients may continue to choose to use it: but the important question here is whether we can really be confident that there is no long-term hazard of any kind associated with a particular treatment. Another important question concerns women's attitudes to different therapies, and we will therefore draw on information from our miscarriage survey to indicate how women feel about the various methods doctors are currently using to try to prevent miscarriage. In the final chapter we look at the attitudes held by a group of doctors towards the various managements.

Hormone treatment

Hormones have been used in the treatment of threatened miscarriage for many years. The two main groups of hormones are progestogens and oestrogens. Progesterone, as we have already mentioned, has been thought of as the true 'pregnancy maintenance' hormone; the hormone that keeps the inside of the uterus quiet and stops it contracting too violently until normal labour starts. The evidence for this is not good, and other hormones also fit this bill, but belief (rather than cast-iron evidence) in this theory has led doctors to give progesterone in early pregnancy to women with a history of early miscarriage.

The best way to test the effectiveness of any treatment for preventing recurrent miscarriage is what is called a 'randomized controlled trial'. In this type of study a group of women at high risk of having a miscarriage is divided on a random basis into two sub-groups, one of which is given the treatment, while the other is not. The fate of the pregnancy is then compared in the two groups. A common variation on this approach is to give the second group some other known-not-to-be-effective treatment, called a 'placebo'. If this is done, interpretation of the results is generally easier if neither the patients nor the doctors know who is getting the 'treatment' and who the 'placebo'. (If they do know, this could influence their expectations of what the results will be.)

One problem with evaluating the effectiveness of different treatments for miscarriage is that relatively few of the studies done have been randomized controlled trials. Many have simply given women at risk of miscarriage the treatment in question and then quoted a 'success rate' – say 60 per cent. The trouble here is that no one knows how many of the women given the treatment would have gone on to have successful pregnancies without it. As we showed in chapter 1, even after three miscarriages a woman stands at least a 60 per cent chance of having a healthy baby in her next pregnancy – *without treatment of any kind*. This high 'spontaneous cure rate' is a problem for those who are evaluating the success of treatment – though not, of course, for women worrying about repeated miscarriage, for whom it can only be a source of comfort!

Trials of progesterone treatment in the prevention of miscarriage have shown no real benefit from use of this hormone. Giving progesterone does not raise women's chances overall of keeping the pregnancies. Indeed, those trials which have included a 'placebo' group have shown almost equal 'benefit' from use of the placebo. The design of such studies of course cannot distinguish pregnancies with abnormal fetuses from those with normal fetuses, since the condition of the fetus is not known until it leaves the mother's body. It is theoretically possible that treatments such as progesterone might be effective in preventing the miscarriage of normal fetuses in a selected group of women, but we simply do not know.

Another hormone which has been tried is human chorionic gonadotrophin (HCG). This has been given to women who threaten to miscarry, in the hope that it will make the corpus luteum produce more progesterone to help maintain the pregnancy. But no proper trials have been completed to date to assess the value of giving HCG in early pregnancy, and, despite optimistic claims by some enthusiasts, the results of studies so far are not really convincing, especially as measurements of HCG in women who go on to miscarry have never shown a lack of this hormone. So, although in theory one might believe that this is the very first hormonal signal of pregnancy failure, it would seem that it is an extremely rare cause of miscarriage, if a cause at all.

There are many other hormones being produced in early pregnancy and a deficiency of any of them could be considered possibly to cause failure of the continuation of pregnancy. A candidate might be the oestrogens, although paradoxically these hormones make the muscle of the womb tighten or contract, i.e., they have the opposite effect from progesterone. The oestrogens have been tested in clinical trials to see if they might prevent miscarriages. In the early 1950s the synthetic substitute for oestrogen, stilboestrol, was given to women in early pregnancy in several trials in the United States and in this country, but no benefit was shown. In fact, the evidence in one trial suggested that the women given stilboestrol miscarried more often than the controls not given the drug. Not only did the oestrogens do no good, but they have now been shown, many years later, to have done positive harm, as some of the offspring of the women given this drug developed an extremely rare cancer of the vagina, developed abnormalities of their reproductive organs, had fertility problems, and increased problems with their own pregnancies. Abnormalities were not detected in the babies at birth and took 15–20 years to reveal themselves. Although this drug stilboestrol is not given to pregnant women today, the lesson of the past should not be forgotten and should serve only to emphasize that drugs imitating the action of hormones may be dangerous to the fetus in early pregnancy – and that the dangers may not become apparent until years later.

However, despite the lack of evidence for the effectiveness (and safety) of hormone treatments for preventing miscarriages, hormones are still given by some doctors, as was shown by some of the women in our survey who had had more than one actual or threatened miscarriage. One woman, who had lost her previous pregnancy at eight weeks, wrote:

I am at present 22 weeks pregnant and I had a threatened miscarriage at six weeks and ten weeks, both times going into hospital for rest. I have also been on Duphaston [progestogen] tablets since six weeks, and finish taking them this week, so I wondered if they had helped me carry on with this pregnancy and that my problem is hormonal, which was not noticed quickly enough in my first pregnancy to try and save it.

It's hard to know the answer to questions like this. However, there is some evidence that if a woman believes a treatment is doing her some good, then it may well actually have that effect. That the explanation is psychological rather than physical doesn't really matter if the outcome is a healthy child (which is probably the reason why clinical trials of hormones that compared their effect with that of a 'placebo' find the placebo equally beneficial: it's believing that something helpful is being done which counts).

Some women change their doctors after one or more miscarriages in an attempt to secure better treatment, and in these cases the treatment is likely to consist of a more sympathetic and interested attitude on the part of the doctor, in combination with some method such as hormonal supplementation. Marilyn Ostler lost one pregnancy at eleven weeks and in her next pregnancy went to see a well-known consultant gynaecologist and infertility specialist privately.

The consultant and my GP took great care of me for the first eighteen weeks. I had private hormone tests and complete bedrest at home, as I was getting pains as in the previous pregnancy from six to fourteen weeks. The consultant said my progesterone levels remained high and

I was probably carrying a girl this time and would keep it. If the level had fallen, he was going to inject me with HCG. I had two injections of this; to help me conceive at twelve days; and to help the egg become embedded at eighteen days.

At the time of writing Marilyn was still awaiting the birth. Obviously it had made her feel a great deal better to be receiving concerned care from the same doctor throughout pregnancy, and to feel that he, as well, had a personal interest in seeing the pregnancy through to a successful conclusion. But no one knows whether the monitoring and addition to her hormone levels she received as part of the 'package' really did the trick. There is, of course, no evidence that private medical care as opposed to NHS care has anything more to offer in terms of treatment.

It has been pointed out that it is in fact naive to think that deficiency of one hormone would be responsible for early pregnancy loss; after all, there are many different hormones being produced by the corpus luteum and by the fetus and placenta, all interacting with each other. In the meantime the best advice is probably to be cautious about taking hormones in early pregnancy, as there is as yet no good evidence that they are beneficial in preventing miscarriage, and positive evidence that some have done harm in the past.

The treatment of cervical incompetence

In a normal pregnancy the neck of the womb or cervix is a ring which has the ability to remain closed until the birth is imminent, when it dilates enormously. The closed cervix helps keep the fetus and baby inside the womb. But sometimes the cervix does not work properly and relaxes too early. This is called cervical 'incompetence'. Estimates of the frequency with which cervical incompetence occurs vary from one in 100 to one in 2000 pregnancies; these different estimates probably reflect differences both in the groups of women looked at and the definitions of cervical incompetence used in the different studies. Some people feel there is little evidence that the condition exists at all.

Cervical incompetence may be a condition you are born with, or it may be associated with some preceding trauma to the cervix. Occasionally this can happen during a D & C when the opening of the cervix is stretched with a dilator and some of the muscle and connecting tissue cells might be torn.* Damage to the cervix may sometimes also occur during childbirth, and an incompetent cervix is more common in twin or multiple pregnancies, presumably because there is greater pressure on the cervix from having two or more fetuses inside the womb. It may sound as if it would be easy to know whether the cervix is functioning properly or not, but in practice it is quite difficult, as we will see later when trying to assess whether treatment should be used and whether it works. Accurate diagnosis is, however, the most important thing, and two new promising ways of investigating cervical incompetence are by studies of the elasticity of the cervix between pregnancies, and using ultrasound to give a picture of the cervical canal during pregnancy. Both methods are still under evaluation.

When making a diagnosis of cervical incompetence your doctor will use several different clues. One will be the history of your previous pregnancies, because if, for instance, you have lost one or more babies during the middle three months of pregnancy and the baby was normal, it makes it more likely that cervical incompetence was the cause. Another clue the doctor will use is to look directly at your cervix during pregnancy with a speculum which, though occasionally uncomfortable, is perfectly safe. If there is cervical incompetence, the cervix, instead of being tightly closed, will look slightly open and the membranes surrounding the baby might be bulging through. Figure 7.1 shows an 'incompetent' alongside a 'competent' cervix.

With an incompetent cervix, if the membranes surrounding the baby burst, then it is likely that you will

* See page 69–70.

Normal cervix

Incompetent cervix

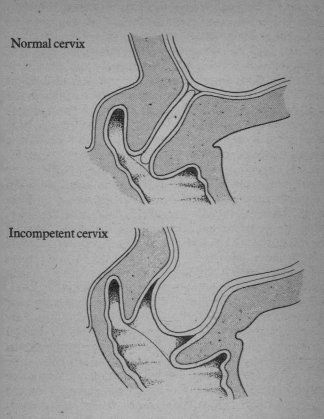

Figure 7.1 **Diagrammatic representation of normal and incompetent cervix**

miscarry. Unfortunately, however, doctors cannot always tell for certain if cervical incompetence exists just by looking at the cervix, because it can be slightly dilated and still perfectly normal if you have had previous pregnancies. Other bits of evidence that may help the doctor are from the history. For example, if you've had an induced abortion, or an operation necessitating the dilatation of the cervix for other reasons, or a previous pregnancy ending in forceps delivery or the birth of a very big baby, the doctor is more likely to suspect incompetence to be a problem. (It would be wrong to get the impression that induced abortion frequently leads to this problem. The techniques used to terminate a pregnancy, and the stage in pregnancy at which the abortion is done, are important considerations: see pages 69–70.

Over the years, a variety of different techniques have been used to treat cervical incompetence. The basis for most of them is to put a thread or stitch into the cervix once pregnancy has been diagnosed, pulling it tight so as to tie the whole thing up like the drawstring of a purse, to stop the fetus falling out. The thread has then to be removed before labour starts normally. The two methods of putting a stitch in the cervix most commonly used are known as a Shirodkar suture and a McDonald suture, after the gynaecologists who developed the techniques. Some doctors put the thread in during early pregnancy, while others prefer to wait until after the third month; the precise positioning of the thread in the cervix by the doctor also varies. Some guide to the way doctors vary in their use of cervical suture is provided by a survey done in Britain by the Medical Research Council. This showed that while some obstetricians never used stitches, others put them in at the rate of one for every 12–13 pregnancies they managed.

In theory, putting a stitch in the cervix sounds a sensible way of preventing miscarriage due to an incompetent cervix, but in practice it is not – alas – so clear cut. In the first place, the actual diagnosis of the condition is very difficult to make, and in the second, inserting the stitch may itself lead to problems. Another theoretical consideration is that if the suture is put in too early it may stop the miscarriage of an abnormal fetus which is obviously not a good idea. Complications include damage to the cervix caused by the stitch itself, infection in the cervix, and bleeding with the insertion of the stitch. Overall, each of these complications is unusual and one should not get them out of proportion, but there is clearly a need for some better way of telling whether or not cervical incompetence is the problem, so that treatment can then be suited to the individual woman's need.

At the moment there are many thousands of women who have had stitches put into their cervices during pregnancy, but there is little published research available from which the balance of benefits and hazards of the procedure can be assessed with any confidence. The studies that have been carried out are conflicting, with one study showing better results (reduced miscarriages) in women who had the stitch put in, while another study showed no difference. In this latter study, women expecting twins were divided into three groups: one group had the stitches, the second did not, and the third group was advised to rest in bed. There were no apparent differences due to the different modes of treatment. None of the studies done to date are randomized controlled trials of cervical suture, although there is such a study now in progress in Britain. Until the results of such research become available, the best advice appears to be that if there is any question of your having a stitch, try to discuss the pros and cons of this with your obstetrician first.

Stitch insertion and removal

If, after consultation, it is decided that the insertion of a stitch is appropriate treatment, what will then be involved? You will have to go into hospital and the stitch will be put in. Usually this will be done under a general anaesthetic, but occasionally it will be done using an epidural anaesthetic. If you have a general anaesthetic, you will obviously feel nothing, but if you have an epidural then you will be awake

153

and, although you won't feel pain, you may feel some pushing and pulling as the doctor puts the stitch in. The stitch is made of heavy silk or Mersiline tape and its exact positioning depends on the individual doctor's technique – some putting it higher up in the cervix than others. The insertion itself doesn't usually take very long. You will be kept in bed for the first 24 hours and discharged after 48 hours if there are no complications. Once the suture is in place, you should lead a normal pregnant life. A small part of the thread from the stitch hangs down out of the cervix into the vagina (rather like that from coil contraception) and if you have intercourse your partner may be aware of it. The only other symptom you may have is increased vaginal discharge. This often continues until the stitch is removed, and there is no way of treating or stopping it. If, however, the discharge is smelly, let your doctor know to make sure there is no infection. If there is any infection, you will need some treatment.

One important thing to remember is that the stitch should be removed before or as soon as you go into labour. It is therefore essential to tell your doctor if you do go into labour or start having any contractions or your waters break before the stitch is removed, otherwise serious complications and injuries to the womb are possible.

When it is time for the stitch to be taken out, and this usually happens at about 38 weeks of pregnancy, you will have to go into hospital again, but this time you will not need a general anaesthetic. The doctor will examine you internally with a speculum and the stitch will be removed by undoing or cutting the knot and pulling it out. You will not necessarily have to stay in hospital, but removing the stitch sometimes starts the womb contracting or breaks the waters and you may go into labour. Many women will carry on with the pregnancy and only deliver at the full 40 weeks or more.

You may know women who were diagnosed as having an incompetent cervix, had a stitch inserted, and then went on either to lose the baby again or to have a successful pregnancy. We did not ask about treatment for incompetent cervix in our miscarriage survey, but several women mentioned it and their experiences were diverse. One mother had a total success story after 3 miscarriages:

> When the doctors did investigations they discovered an incompetent womb, but the doctors couldn't agree whether or not it was bad enough to warrant a stitch. Thankfully, the doctor who looked after me thought it best [to have a stitch put in]! I now have a cheeky little boy . . ..

While another woman's encounter with a cervical stitch was less happy:

> At first it was thought that I had a weak cervix, so when I fell pregnant again, I had a stitch put into the neck of the womb. But again at 25 weeks I went into premature labour.

Bedrest

By far the most common 'treatment' to prevent miscarriage is bedrest. The theory underlying bedrest is that if a woman prone to miscarriage lies as still and as horizontal as possible, her uterus will receive the least possible stimulation and can thus perhaps be persuaded to hold on to the fetus. For many years bedrest either at home or in hospital has been accepted in Britain and other countries as an integral part of the way obstetricians treat many different groups of high-risk pregnancies. Thus, women with raised blood pressure, multiple pregnancies, a history of previous miscarriage or pre-term delivery may all be advised to rest at home, or be admitted to hospital to encourage them to do so.

Many women's initial reaction to the first signs of threatened miscarriage is to go to bed and stay there until the bleeding stops: 'On each occasion (three in all) I rested totally to try and save the pregnancy.' This also seems to be common advice handed out by GPs and consultant obstetricians to women threatening to miscarry:

> At the first sign of blood, I referred to my doctor, who advised bedrest for 24 hours. This I did for 48 hours and all bleeding had ceased. Three days later after taking things easy, the miscarriage occurred.

On the other hand, the advice to rest in bed may be associated with the preservation of the pregnancy, as Dawn Carter found:

> During my first pregnancy, I had a slight show. I rang the doctor who didn't call to see me, but advised me to have 48 hours' bedrest. This I did, and the pregnancy progressed to full term with no ill effects. The baby was born perfectly normal.

Quite a few of the women who completed our questionnaires felt that their GPs could have done more for them than merely advise bedrest (usually only via the telephone):

> When I had my first miscarriage I called my doctor. He told me to take an aspirin and go to bed and call him in the morning, if I was still losing, which I did. He then said bedrest would put it right. At 8 o'clock in the evening I started losing clots as big as the palm of your hand. My husband rang the doctor and he reluctantly came out, which was the first time since I first phoned at 8 o'clock the night before.

However, a speedier response on the part of Rosemary Allen's GP in her next pregnancy didn't improve matters and she miscarried again. The third time round: 'I threatened to miscarry at thirteen weeks in Harbury Hospital. They let me see her on a scan and they said there was nothing wrong with her.' This reassurance seemed to help and the baby was born healthy and normal.

As with the beneficial psychological effect of hormone injections mentioned earlier (pages 145–9), if you *believe* that bedrest is a good thing it may do you some good. A number of women attributed their eventual success in keeping a pregnancy to 'excellent, personal care' by a particular consultant, who often recommended bedrest as well. For example, 'I would just like to say', wrote one woman, 'that I think my eventually having my little girl came about largely because I am fortunate enough to have a consultant obstetrician who always allocates a few beds for bedrest. I was on *total* bedrest for three and a half months, and I'm sure this got me over the critical period.'

The great advantage of bedrest as a treatment for threatened miscarriage is that it is relatively harmless, although, of course, being asked to remain in bed for long periods of time will interfere with other aspects of one's life. It's difficult to see how bedrest could prevent the miscarriage of an abnormal fetus, or one that is already dead. As we have said, ultrasound may be useful to help sort out whether or not it's even worth considering going to bed. We would add a cautionary note to the effect that those women unable to rest (because, for example, they already have children to care for) should not feel guilty if they don't go to bed and do go on to miscarry. The effectiveness of bedrest as a treatment has never been properly evaluated, though it looks as though one such study may get off the ground soon. Because of this, we lack the right kind of evidence to assess the real value of bedrest. One study, not a clinical trial, was done in the 1950s, and this analysed women threatening to miscarry into three groups: one group had been hospitalized and put to bed, one group had had partial bedrest at home and the third group had been advised to lead normal lives. Out of the hospitalized group, 59 per cent miscarried, of those who rested at home 81 per cent had miscarriages, while 54 per cent of the women who led normal lives went on to miscarry. Although the women in the three groups were not strictly comparable, this study does not suggest any obvious benefit from bedrest in its ability to prevent miscarriage.

Rhesus blood groups

The treatments discussed so far are all treatments for a threatened miscarriage or for when you get pregnant again. There is one other important aspect of treatment which must not be forgotten, and which only affects women whose blood group is rhesus negative (all human beings have either rhesus positive or rhesus negative blood as well as the ABO blood groups). It is *essential* for those women with rhesus negative blood who miscarry or threaten to miscarry that they be given an injection of Anti-D-gammaglobulin within 72 hours to prevent the formation of antibodies in the mother's bloodstream. Once formed, these antibodies could produce severe complications in a future pregnancy by destroying the baby's red blood cells.

Many women do not know their blood group when they get pregnant. If you know you are rhesus positive and you miscarry, then there is no need to worry about what is said under this heading. If you are rhesus negative and miscarry or threaten to miscarry, it is important to be in touch with your doctor so you can have the Anti-D-gammaglobulin injection. If you do not know your blood group, it's important to tell your doctor about a miscarriage or threatened miscarriage so your blood can be tested and you can have the injection if necessary. You may have to go to a hospital to get the blood test and injection, but sometimes your own GP will be able to do this for you.

Conclusion

Despite the great need for a safe and effective treatment to prevent the miscarriage of normal fetuses, there is, at present, no such general treatment available. This is the conclusion we have reached after surveying the research that's been done. Or, rather, perhaps we should say that we do not yet have the right kind of evidence to show that any of the methods commonly used are both effective and safe. We need more research and, particularly, research of the right kind. The most we can say is do what you feel is best for you. It is important to feel you have done everything you felt was right in order to preserve the pregnancy. Finally, we believe that there is plenty of evidence to show that humane personal care and social support from medical staff make women facing the threat of miscarriage feel a great deal more comfortable.

8 Trying Again

All that was said was, 'Never mind, better luck next time!'

As we have already observed in this book, having a miscarriage may not be a trivial experience, and one of the ways in which it is not trivial lies in its capacity to influence attitudes towards future pregnancies. Indeed, the experience of having a miscarriage may very well make a woman realize for the first time just where in her list of priorities pregnancy and motherhood really are. If she conceived easily, according to plan, losing the baby may impress on her that the simple biological achievements of womanhood are not so simple after all. It may seem that nature, not the individual's own wishes, determines who shall be successful in the race to become a mother, and for those of us who have grown up in an era preaching the importance (and possibility) of self-determination for women, this is a hard lesson to learn. Perhaps it was not so difficult for our grandmothers to accept miscarriage as a part of women's lives which does not need to bring that crushing sense of personal failure described by some women:

> [I felt] very depressed and a personal failure, worried the same thing would happen the next time, but I wanted to try again.

> I felt the need to have a child more than before I had the miscarriage – I think just to prove that I could have another child.

This, of course, is not to say that a feeling of personal failure

160

is a necessary accompaniment to miscarriage. Some women are able to take a more optimistic view:

> Although I had a miscarriage, I wasn't particularly worried by it. I know it is very common to have miscarriages – nearly all my friends had at least one, as had my mother. It didn't occur to me that I would have any difficulty the next time round.

The whole situation is more complex when conception has been, and remains, hard to achieve. After her miscarriage, Maria Saunders, for example, said she was 'Devastated. It had taken me five years to get pregnant. The doctors treated it as an everyday event and just tough luck.' Of course it isn't easy for doctors to know, unless you tell them, that a miscarriage is likely to be extra-devastating because of the infertility preceding it, and because of the anticipation that it may take a long time to get pregnant again.

Even for the most 'liberated woman', miscarriage can seem like failing as a woman. Thus, the post-miscarriage reaction of wanting to 'prove' oneself capable of successful pregnancy may occur even if one already has children. Unsuccessful pregnancy can disturb previously held ideas about oneself as a 'good reproducer', and is almost as shocking as the panic reaction of those still childless. One of our survey mothers, Celia Reading, described as 'ridiculous and self-indulgent' her misery at a six-week miscarriage when 'I already had two children, a job, a husband etc. etc.' and her own surprise at the strength of her desire to have another baby – to 'try again' in that commonly used phrase, which hardly seems to do justice to the emotional and physical magnitude of what one is trying to do. Most of the women who filled in our questionnaires described this response of immediately wanting another pregnancy: 'I felt desperate to become pregnant again immediately, in spite of the worry of having another miscarriage.' There can of course be other reactions, as Sally Farr found, after her third miscarriage:

Immediately after my most recent miscarriage my thoughts were that I could never go through all that again, and we decided to put our names forward for adoption. But after a week I was once again ready to have another go at having our own child . . . Honestly, I think I will try for as long as is either needed or possible.

'A far cry from the liberated woman'

One of the problems with deciding to 'try again' is that the pursuit of successful pregnancy can come to dominate one's life. This is especially so if there is difficulty in conceiving, or further miscarriages. Veronica Newson had a healthy daughter in 1957 and then six miscarriages in the years up to 1970, all early ones. In 1964, after the first two miscarriages, and being dissatisfied with the lack of continuity of care she was getting in NHS clinics, she decided to see a consultant privately. He diagnosed and treated a cervical infection, admitted her to hospital to 'blow my tubes', and began a course of hormone injections. After the next four miscarriages she removed herself to the care of another private consultant, 'the biggest name I knew'. She put it to him that if there was any hope, any point in continuing to try for another child, she would do so, but otherwise the upheavals connected with even the 'easiest' of her miscarriages made her feel she was allowing the pursuit of successful pregnancy too big a part in her life:

My daughter was thirteen and had seen me in bed for quite a lot of her life. Mr H. said he could probably deliver a baby but I would need to spend most of the pregnancy in bed in hospital. I decided my family had taken enough.

As well as the burden on her family for the whole of the period during which she tried for her second child, her job had to take what was very much second place:

I was a research worker before all this. In between bouts I took teaching jobs but decided I could not responsibly take on A level classes while deliberately trying to get pregnant. This means I now have a very lowly job which sometimes makes me feel rather jealous when I meet others I used to know.

This unplanned train of events in which having children occupies many years, instead of months, can be very difficult to survive emotionally. 'I sometimes feel that my view of the world is distorted,' wrote one woman, 'I know that only the conclusion of a successful pregnancy of my own will cure the situation.' Or, as Wanda Phillips reported:

By the time I'd experienced two early miscarriages and a thirteen-week miscarriage, I felt really stupid. Endless days off work for pregnancies which were not apparent made me feel totally inadequate, as if I'd imagined it all and was just neurotic – a far cry from this liberated pregnant women I'd expected to be . . .

The next pregnancy: how long should I wait?

In table 8.1 we show the medical advice given to the women in our survey about when to try to start their next pregnancy after a miscarriage. As an aside, we would note that many women *only* receive advice about pregnancy spacing when they would have liked more in the way of post-miscarriage counselling:

Neither my GP nor hospital seemed to consider it necessary to advise or inform me in any way other than to suggest that it might be a good idea to wait two months before becoming pregnant again.

Table 8.1 **How long were you advised to wait before starting another pregnancy?**

	%
Get pregnant straight away	4
1 month	8
2 months	16
3 months	57
4 months or more	13
2 years*	2
Total % receiving advice	81

*These women had a hydatidiform mole (see page 20)

Four out of five women (81 per cent) were given specific advice about the timing of the next pregnancy, and the most common time quoted was three months. There seems to be no rational basis for this advice, in that we have no good evidence for supposing that the outlook for the next pregnancy is better if the time between pregnancies is three rather than one or six months. Women are usually advised to wait for at least one normal period after a miscarriage in order to be able accurately to date the next pregnancy should it happen. And of course if you do not feel ready either physically or emotionally for another pregnancy then it is best to give yourself more time.

However 'ready' you are for your next pregnancy after a miscarriage, you will probably not be able to embark on it without at least some anxiety. It's helpful to recognize this and work out ways of coping with it in advance. Talking to other women in a similar predicament is probably most important:

When I became pregnant again and started going to NCT classes it was almost with a huge sense of relief that three other first time mothers and I discovered that we'd all had miscarriages! Now we could talk about it, but it really was a bit late. We all felt that more help should have been available at the time. There really had been no one, apart from our partners, whom any of us felt we could turn to. You really can't believe that everything will be all right next time. My doubts remained with me right up until my baby's birth.

While for another woman,

When I knew Joanne was on the way, it was nine months of hell. No reassurance, no support and no one to answer my questions. The GP was hopeless and the midwife never there. I saw the consultant once for five minutes. I didn't see anyone until thirteen weeks – my GP said when I went for a pregnancy test: 'Come back in four weeks if you're still pregnant.'

Will it happen again?

It's important here to emphasize a point we made earlier: that most women after a miscarriage will go on to have a normal baby. The chances of miscarrying again are slightly raised if you have had one miscarriage. If one takes the likelihood of miscarriage happening in any pregnancy as 15–20 per cent, then the likelihood of having a subsequent miscarriage, having already had one or two previous miscarriages, probably increases to about 25 per cent. Putting it the other way round, after one miscarriage you have a 75 per cent chance of having a normal pregnancy, as opposed to an 80–85 per cent chance if you haven't had a miscarriage. The risk of a repeat miscarriage may be slightly greater if you have never had a live baby before, and slightly lower if you have. We have put some of the available figures on the chances of repeat miscarriage in tables 8.2 and 8.3.

Table 8.2 **The risk of having a repeat miscarriage**

Number of past miscarriages	% next pregnancies that miscarry
0	15–20
1	24
2	26
3	32
4 or more	32

Table 8.3 **Chances of successful pregnancy following miscarriage**

Number of past miscarriages	% next pregnancies that do not miscarry
0	80–85
1	76
2	74
3	68
4 or more	68

As we can see from the first of these tables, if you have had three or four miscarriages the chances of miscarrying again are about one in three. Putting the figures the other way around (table 8.3), we can see that the chances of successful pregnancy following miscarriage are really quite high – 76 per cent of women who've had one miscarriage will succeed with their next pregnancies, and even after four or more 68 per cent of women will have normal pregnancies the next time.

If the fetus of the first miscarriage has some *chromosomal abnormality*, it seems that you are less likely to miscarry the second time around. Conversely, if you have a miscarriage of a *chromosomally normal* fetus, then you are slightly more likely to have a miscarriage the second time around. The rationale behind this is that the chromosome abnormality by itself is more likely to have happened just by chance, and is unlikely to happen again, but when there is a miscarriage with no chromosomal abnormality, it may be due to other factors (hormonal, structural, etc.) that are less understood and perhaps rather more likely to recur.

The exception to this rule of a repeat miscarriage being less likely after the loss of a chromosomally abnormal, rather than normal, fetus is that a few parents possess chromosomal abnormalities in their own cells which they may pass on to their fetuses, and these *are* more likely to recur. If you do have recurrent miscarriages (by this we mean two or three consecutive ones), then examination of your and your partner's chromosomes may help to sort out the problem. There are also a very few chromosomal abnormalities that have a habit of recurring spontaneously in the fetus for reasons we are not yet clear about, and in these cases examination of the fetus may help. Some 5 per cent of couples experiencing recurrent miscarriage will be found to have a chromosomal cause in either the man or the woman.

The high chance of a successful pregnancy following miscarriage means that there is good reason to look on the bright side and believe everything *will* be all right this time. Yet believing this oneself is a lot harder than merely saying it, especially in the middle of the night, or after a few drinks one feels one should not have had, or when a spot or two of blood or a few 'twinges' suggest that the same disaster is about to strike again.

Bleeding in early pregnancy: what does it mean?

In a pregnancy which follows a miscarriage, a particular worry may be the significance of any bleeding that does occur. The first thing to say is that bleeding in pregnancy does not inevitably mean miscarriage (see pages 86–7). We should also mention here what is known about pregnancy bleeding in relation to the outcome of pregnancy. The national survey of British births that was done in 1970 found that some 10 per cent of women giving birth during the survey period reported some vaginal bleeding in pregnancy, and most of these women delivered normal live babies. Looking at all the studies that have been done of the incidence of pregnancy bleeding, it seems that reported rates of bleeding vary from one in 100 to 20 in 100 pregnancies depending on the study. Most of this twentyfold variation is likely to be due to differences in methods of reporting or defining bleeding. Some studies only included women who had had very severe bleeds, and were therefore admitted to hospital – in which case one would expect a low rate – while others included women who only bled slightly in which case one would expect a high rate.

Whether the bleeding is light or heavy, and whether it is accompanied by pain or not, will obviously determine what percentage of women who bleed carry on and have a miscarriage, as against those who bleed but continue with the pregnancy. Among women who bleed enough to be admitted to hospital, some 50–60 per cent end up with a miscarriage. This is sometimes described as a threatened miscarriage going on to an inevitable miscarriage (see pages 83–8). We cannot know accurately from published data how many women who bleed are admitted to hospital, as this will depend on many factors, including both women's own social attitudes and circumstances, and their doctor's attitude to bleeding in pregnancy; whether they've had bleeding in a previous pregnancy; and whether this has ended in miscarriage or a normal delivery. In general it is fair to say that the heavier the bleeding the more likely it is that a miscarriage will finally result.

But what happens if you bleed and do not miscarry? There are two things to consider here. One is the question of whether the baby is more likely to have a congenital abnormality. On this score it is possible to be very reassuring. If you have no bleeding complications in pregnancy the chances of delivering a baby with no congenital abnormalities is 95.5 per cent. If you have had some bleeding in the first three months of pregnancy, then the chances of having a baby with no congenital abnormality are 95 per cent. If you have some bleeding in the second three months then the chances of having a baby with no congenital abnormalities are 94.3 per cent, and with bleeding in the last three months it is 95.3 per cent. From this it can be seen that in fact bleeding in pregnancy has very little association with an increased chance of having a baby with a congenital abnormality.

However, congenital abnormalities (i.e., physical and biochemical problems arising during the course of pregnancy, typical examples of which are Down's syndrome, spina bifida, cleft lip, etc.), are not the only possible complications. For instance, babies may be born very prematurely, or the wrong way round (breech), or very small for the length of the pregnancy, or they may die in the time around birth.

Once again we are faced with the problem that different studies show conflicting results. While some suggest that threatened miscarriage does not predispose to these other pregnancy complications, other studies show an up to three-fold increase in the likelihood of all these factors.

To summarize these studies, it could be said that bleeding in early pregnancy is associated with miscarriage, the likelihood of miscarriage depending on the severity of bleeding. The risk of congenital abnormality does not seem to be significantly affected, but the outcome of pregnancy as far as the prematurity and death of the baby is concerned is slightly less certain. Perhaps because of this it would seem wise that where heavy bleeding has occurred early in pregnancy, extra care should be taken in watching the progress of pregnancy and delivery. Although we do not know for certain, it seems unlikely that the same caution is necessary following very light bleeding in pregnancy.

Denial, anxiety and disbelief

One common way in which women cope with the anxiety of another pregnancy after one which has miscarried is by denying that they are pregnant. Carole Saunders's experience, quoted on pages 29–36, shows this reaction clearly. Celia Reading found herself having the same reaction in a pregnancy following a six-week miscarriage, despite the fact that she already had two healthy children and therefore some confidence in her body to be pregnant successfully. Because her description is reminiscent of many we received, we quote it in full:

> I turned away all thoughts of the pregnancy, deliberately not working out when it would be born, refusing to let my eyes stray towards baby clothes, etc., but, at the same time, ridiculously, swimming more slowly, not running for buses as a protective measure, and trying to be unaware of that bloated feeling, and feeling guilty and tearful every time I did forget and cheerfully knock back a few drinks. Every time I went to the loo I experienced the rush of fear that I was bleeding and relief that I wasn't.
>
> Luckily, for most of these very early stages I was very busy with all sorts of absorbing things to do, but on long bus journeys it was impossible not to think and hope about the pregnancy. I was torn between making it official by telling the doctor quite early (perhaps in the last few months some magic way of preventing miscarriage had been found?) and believing that it would be tempting fate. James and I both lived in this unreal state of unspoken anxiety and delight.

In the end the temptation to share it was too great, and she told her GP:

> I almost asked him not to write it on my notes . . . fate

again. He was much more cheerful than me and more optimistic. 'After all, what about the law of averages?' Anyway I was pregnant and that must be a good thing. No there wasn't anything much I could do to keep it safe. The riskiest times were when one's period was due up until about the thirteenth week. Going on the boat for a holiday was the perfect sort of holiday to have. He would just put a very small note in my notes about it . . .

All that did not make me less anxious, and I did not believe the hopeful noises but it did *delight* me. I nearly danced down the street and later that day James and I allowed ourselves a small slice of that delight. I can well see the foolishness of early rejoicing and pretence that everything will go well. It's hard to think of the best approach for doctors, relatives and the pregnant. I know that denial is in part a protection but I do not now think it is the whole story. I was heartened by my GPs reaction, perhaps I even relaxed a bit, but I certainly didn't believe everything would be all right. I am glad and grateful he did react as he did, especially since I subsequently found it was a rather rare reaction. If I had or do miscarry I do not think it will have made it worse. As with stillbirth and death, I begin to think that if pregnancies are longed for they have to be acknowledged when they occur, with all the conflicting emotions that means.

Most of the summer on the boat I slept, to the consternation or amusement of everyone but James, who was the only person in the know. That was punctuated by endless trips to the loo, a foul taste in my mouth, an aversion to most foods and, despite that, the feeling of being, and in fact getting, enormously fat. Weeks 8 and 12 were frightening and I made all sorts of efforts not to be too dramatically busy at that time. During the day I blotted out all thoughts of the baby and when I didn't James did it for me by being quite scolding, which in fact helped. But at night the controls were off. These were the results:

Nearly every night for several weeks I would dream just

before I woke that I had miscarried. I would then wake and lie too frightened to see if it was true. I would feel to see if I was bleeding and if I was at all sticky would not look any further. When I had to get out of bed I would hardly dare go to the loo to find out the awful truth.

On other nights, although not so often, the dream would be more elaborate. I would have definitely miscarried but there was a chance that the baby was not dead. This is because I had put it in a safe warm place to incubate. I would then in the dream hunt all over the house clearing out the airing cupboard, looking in the oven and even in the cat's basket. I never found it and would get more and more desperate and usually wake crying. The worst part of it, which may say some interesting things about people needing to see the fetus, is that I did not mind so much about finding a dead fetus, but I could not bear finding nothing.

On another occasion, following a visit to the GP at which the question of where she might have the baby was discussed, Celia had a different dream:

I was having the baby on a very high table in an operating theatre under enormous bright lights. Just like before. However, the difference was that I was so enormous that the doctors *et al* had to stand on ladders to get at me. Despite my size they could not seem to find a baby and eventually fetched spades to dig around to see if they could get it out, if indeed it was there. At this point I woke sobbing and feeling afraid. It was marvellous to find myself in a nice warm bed with James in a dark room and only a little larger than normal.

I did not dream after the first thirteen weeks, except for once before the amniocentesis. The baby had been born prematurely but was apparently perfectly all right. I hadn't seen it and didn't much want to but was persuaded. It was in a perfectly ordinary cot and I was told I could nurse it. Again, I didn't want to although I was told it was perfectly all right. When I picked it up it was rather hairy and had only stubby little legs and arms. I can't remember feeling upset at all. I just went away and never came back.

Since then nothing except the once or twice a day wave of panic that I may still miscarry, or there will be a stillbirth, and then maybe a cot death. Oh God, I used to be such a calm collected and together pregnant person . . . !

And she became a calm, collected and together mother – for the third time, when her daughter was born healthy and at the right time.

Many women sent us 'success' stories:

I had an enjoyable pregnancy with no problems to speak of, a quick labour (5 hours) which I enjoyed, and a lovely little boy at the end of it.

I would just like to tell you I have now a beautiful daughter who is four months old. I conceived her just one month after my second miscarriage.

I was pleased it only took four months to conceive again, although I was worried about the possibility of it recurring. However, I was lucky to have a trouble-free pregnancy and now a daughter who is extra precious . . .

We now have a lovely daughter and although the pregnancy was wonderful, I still couldn't believe that I wasn't going to miscarry again, and only when she was placed in my arms did I finally accept that all was well.

When I again conceived I hoped all through my pregnancy for a boy to replace, at it were, the one I had lost and I was lucky enough to have my prayers answered. I gave birth to a healthy boy exactly a year later and had fantastic treatment in hospital from the staff who had remembered me from the previous year.

Some women are wary from the start of this feeling that the new baby will replace the lost one, sensing that this does not happen and indeed is a bad idea for the new baby's sake. Thus Marilyn Lewis recalls:

> . . . my subsequent pregnancy was undertaken with very great trepidation, and the first seven months of pregnancy were a worrying time. When this baby was born, it became apparent that my previous, barely conscious feelings that this baby would 'make up' for the lost baby were completely erroneous. The new baby is another individual in its own right and the baby that was lost can never be simply replaced.

As she indicates, it is sensible to be aware of the fact that the emotional impact of miscarriage may endure not only to mould a woman's attitudes to the next pregnancy, but beyond that to her relationship with the new baby:

> During my ensuing successful pregnancy, I had no anticipation of, nor preparation for, my forthcoming child: neither did I have any emotional reaction to my baby until she was about six months old.

> When I had the baby, I couldn't seem to take in the fact that she was *mine*, and only now, in the past year, have accepted the fact . . . at the time I just felt that, although I loved her, she didn't seem real, or, if she did, I felt that something would happen to her. I think that if I had been able to talk the worries and disappointment and fears 'out of my system' *before* I had got pregnant again, both myself and my baby would have been a lot happier.

Special investigations and tests

Most of us want to understand why things happen to us, and miscarriage is no exception. We feel that if we know why the miscarriage happened, then we are in a much better position to decide whether to get pregnant again. Especially if the cause of the miscarriage is one that is unlikely to be repeated, then coping emotionally with the anxiety of the next pregnancy is easier. Hannah Evans:

> I suppose I was quite lucky in that the doctor looking after me when I had my miscarriage had been able to tell me that the baby had a relatively rare chromosomal abnormality. Sometimes, the abnormalities aren't evident to the naked eye, and it wasn't the hospital's policy to examine the fetus if it was only your first pregnancy. But I was already in my thirties, and I didn't feel able to start another pregnancy until I felt confident that I'd at least stand the same chance as anyone else that it wouldn't happen again. Our GP referred us to a geneticist, and we saw her within a couple of months. She reassured us that the chances of it happening again were minimal, and a year later, we had a healthy baby boy.

So what about the advisability of seeing a geneticist or having other investigations after a miscarriage? Most doctors do not consider it necessary to investigate the cause of miscarriage if a woman has had only one. Their 'policy' is based on the very hopeful statistics quoted earlier, that in most cases the next pregnancy will be all right. Furthermore, for otherwise healthy women having one or two miscarriages in the first twelve weeks of pregnancy, it is generally accepted by most doctors that detailed studies are not necessary or helpful as they do *not* influence the management of future pregnancies. This does not mean, of course, that other forms of treatment in the way of support, explanation and reassurance should be forgotten. Women often find it difficult to accept that special investigations are not necessarily helpful; thus Georgia Turner poignantly asked:

> What worries me is, do I have to lose a second and third baby before anyone will do anything to help me, and find out why I had the miscarriage? If my doctor would only take the time to realize that one baby was one too many for me to lose.

If you are in this situation it's hard to realize that there may be nothing doctors can do to find out why you miscarried or to help stop it happening again. It's much easier to feel the answer is there somewhere, and it's only a question of persuading someone to give it to you: this way you can also feel angry with doctors instead of beginning to come to terms with what has happened and preparing yourself for the extra anxiety of the next pregnancy.

If you have had a lengthy period of infertility in addition to a tendency to miscarry, it would, on the other hand, be wise to pursue the question of what might be accounting for the dual problem. It might be little comfort at the time of your miscarriage, but if you've conceived once, you *can* usually conceive again. If it's taken a long time to get pregnant in the first place, you may feel reluctant to embark on another pregnancy straight away. This was Miranda Cole's feeling:

> We had been trying for a baby for a number of years and I had been on infertility treatment in order to conceive, so it was a terrible shock after all we had been through. I went through every emotion afterwards i.e. sorrow, anger, frustration, despair, failure, which ended up as depression when I carried on with normal life as if on 'automatic pilot', but was empty inside and could show no interest in anything. It was nearly two years before I could consider trying again. It took great courage and 100% support from my husband to start the fertility treatment again. (I am

now 32 weeks pregnant and keeping everything crossed!) I found the NAC* a great comfort; it took away some of the feeling of isolation. I would say that I will never 'get over' my miscarriage, but that I have gradually learnt to live with it, and that the pain lessens as time goes by.

If a woman has had more than two or three miscarriages in the first twelve weeks of pregnancy (known as habitual or recurrent miscarriage), it is a good idea if possible to have the fetus examined for chromosomal and other abnormalities, and to examine both parents for possible abnormalities. With two miscarriages after twelve weeks, a woman's doctor will probably want to arrange further investigations to make sure there is no structural abnormality of the womb or any evidence of cervical incompetence (see pages 149–50). Some doctors will suggest these tests after only one late miscarriage.

The amount, type and timing of the investigations done will vary according to such factors as your age, whether you've had previous normal or abnormal babies, when during pregnancy previous miscarriages have occurred, etc. There are no absolute rules, just general guidelines. How much is done in the way of investigations should be decided by discussion between you and your doctor, bearing these factors in mind.

If you or your doctor think that a chromosomal problem may have caused your miscarriage(s) and should be investigated, your GP can refer you to a geneticist. You can see this specialist within the NHS and he or she will be able to give you some idea of what the statistical chances are of a particular abnormality occurring again. Before going, try to find out from other members of your family about any handicapped children (perhaps born to your grandparents – so you might not have known about them), and try to find out whether other women in your family have had miscarriages or stillbirths, and if any reason was known for these. The geneticist won't be able to tell you whether or not

* National Association for the Childless.

you will miscarry next time, but will be able to give you some idea of the *probability* of particular problems occurring or recurring.

If it does seem likely that there may be a chromosomal problem, the geneticist may suggest you have an amniocentesis done in the next pregnancy. In this procedure a sample of amniotic fluid is withdrawn through the mother's abdominal wall at 15–16 weeks of pregnancy and the cells in the fluid grown in a culture medium in a laboratory to find out the chromosome makeup of the fetus. If there is reason to suspect that the fetus may have a neural tube malformation (spina bifida or anencephaly) then the same test may be done. In this case it will be preceded by a blood test for a substance called alphafetoprotein which shows up in the mother's blood as a 'marker' of fetal abnormalities. These tests can be immensely reassuring to a worried mother, but there are three problems with them. The first and foremost is that it is important to know what you will do if an abnormal fetus is diagnosed. If you are against abortion under any circumstances, then you may not want to have the tests done. They detect abnormalities – they don't cure them.

The second problem is that the amniocentesis test does carry a very slight risk of miscarriage (though this risk is very substantially lessened if the person carrying it out has done a lot of these tests before). Thirdly, the tests in themselves can make you more anxious, so it is important to work out the right balance of benefits and hazards *for you* before agreeing to, or pressing for, such investigations. The same applies to ultrasound scans used to detect fetal abnormalities at a stage in pregnancy permitting termination if necessary. Ultrasound scans were described by some of the mothers in our survey as very encouraging when they displayed a live and healthy fetus to a mother who had miscarried in a previous pregnancy: in this way the mother is put in contact with the reality of a living fetus to sustain her throughout the rest of the pregnancy.

Preconceptional care

In the last few years the idea of special pre-pregnancy care has been put forward as a good idea for all would be parents, but especially for those who have had an unsuccessful pregnancy before. For some reason this 'preconceptional' care has become known as 'preconceptual' care. The basic philosophy underlying it is that healthy babies are most likely to come from healthy parents: thus pregnancy should be preceded by making sure one has a healthy diet, doesn't smoke or drink too much, takes sufficient exercise, is not under too much stress etc.

Irrespective of whether a formal programme of care appeals to you, it does seem to be sensible to make sure that you are in good general health before you become pregnant. An earlier chapter discusses the possible effects of smoking and drinking on the fetus, and since it might be difficult to give these up during pregnancy because it is a stressful time for many women (and worrying may make you want to smoke more, not less) it's worth trying to cut down or give up before getting pregnant. The time before you get pregnant is also a good time to pay some attention to your diet. If you're used to rushing round with only a bar of chocolate at lunchtime, try and get into a routine where you're eating a well-balanced diet with plenty of fruit and vegetables. If you suffered from morning sickness in previous pregnancies, changes in diet may make you feel a bit better. None of these precautions is guaranteed to stop another miscarriage, but they are very unlikely to do any harm, and the psychological effect on you of feeling you have done your best (as with bedrest, page 157) may well help. It is important to mention rubella (german measles) under preconceptional care. Many women now of childbearing age will have had rubella immunization at school. But some will have missed this, and they will not have had the illness itself. Before planning to get pregnant, and even if you think you might have had the disease, it is worth checking with your doctor to see whether or not you are immune to rubella. This can be done with a simple blood test.

Your antenatal care

Most people are relatively happy with their GPs, but if you felt that your doctor wasn't particularly sympathetic when you were having your miscarriage, and you find it difficult to discuss your worries about pregnancy with him or her, it may be worth trying to establish a better relationship before your next pregnancy. If you really feel that this isn't possible, then perhaps you should consider changing your doctor. Ask other mothers in your neighbourhood about good doctors, or if you prefer, you can stay with your family doctor for general medical care, and have another doctor to do your antenatal care. You can get the list of doctors who do antenatal care from your local Family Practitioner Committee (via the Post Office). A possible disadvantage to changing one's doctor after miscarriage is of course precisely the loss of continuity of care and the information about one's medical history that goes with it.

Another difficulty is that in some areas, you will not be booked in for antenatal care at the hospital until about twelve weeks, and will certainly not be seeing someone regularly until quite late on in your pregnancy. Since those first weeks – perhaps before anyone else even knows that you are pregnant, before anything shows, and when you may not be feeling your best – can be particularly hard, it might be worth asking if you can meet your community midwife at an early stage. If you already have young children, your health visitor may be a helpful resource. There *are* helpful people around, it just may be a difficult exercise to find them!

But above all, under the heading of 'trying again' we would say, do what is best *for you*. Don't feel pressured to start another pregnancy straightaway – or to wait longer than feels right. Don't tell anyone you're pregnant at first if that's not what you want to do (many women report a superstitious feeling that telling people early on will bring bad luck). Spend several months adjusting your own and your partner's health before conceiving again if you think that's a good idea. Divert your energies away from motherhood and into other fields if you feel that you are not the sort of person who should put years of effort into trying to have a child. Don't search your conscience all the time for things you may be doing wrong – if you are taking the trouble to read this book then you are hardly likely to be committing any major misdemeanours towards a future child. And, finally, remember you have a good chance of having a healthy baby and of facing the normal trials and tribulations as well as the joys of ordinary parenthood!

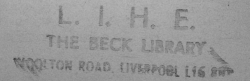

9 Looking Back (But Not So Much in Anger)

'I had to tell you what had happened. I lost the child. It's a simple fact. There is no judgement, there's no blame...'

(Osborne, 1957)

We began this book by pointing out the contradiction between miscarriage as a statistically common, self-curing, reproductive event on the one hand, and, on the other, the intensely private and often traumatic nature of the experience. Early pregnancy loss is a 'normal' part of human reproductive experience. It is equally normal for women who have had a miscarriage also to have successful pregnancies without medical treatment. The condition of miscarriage is, in this sense, usually self-curing, and unlike many other 'illnesses' it rarely threatens a woman's life or generally incapacitates her. Her and her partner's plans for parenthood may be thrown off course, but the fact of miscarriage does not automatically handicap either of them in other areas of life.

Yet these considerations, drawn from statistical analyses of miscarriage, say nothing about its personal dimensions. Not all women, or all couples, react strongly to the event of miscarriage, but for those who do, the statistical frequency and curability of miscarriage may offer poor comfort. Just as there are always some people less fortunate than oneself, there are always some more fortunate, and the world of a woman who has just miscarried is full of victoriously healthy pregnant women and babies. Every miscarriage is a private experience, and every miscarriage is different. But, while there are limits to other people's understanding of such private events, miscarriage is also an experience shared by many women, and we hope we have shown some of the common properties of this experience in earlier chapters.

As we have repeatedly noted throughout the book, what we can say about the incidence, causes, treatment and physical and psychological aftermath of miscarriage is severely limited by the lack of appropriate research. For example, our calculations of the annual incidence of miscarriage in Britain (page 12) had to be an estimate based on the number of live births, special studies of the frequency of miscarriage among married women, figures for hospital discharges of women treated for miscarriages, and the annual returns of GPs claiming for attending miscarrying women. There is no research which can easily generate an accurate figure. In the same way we have had to discuss the different possible treatments for miscarriage without knowing anything about how many women in Britain today are receiving which form of treatment. In discussing the psychological consequences of miscarriage we have also tapped an obviously incomplete literature, for the views of those responding most traumatically to miscarriage are over-represented in any survey (including our own) which is not based on a random sample of all women experiencing miscarriage. Nonetheless, given these constraints, we hope we have produced a reasonably balanced picture.

A conspiracy of silence?

Writing this book we had to confront the question of why miscarriage has for so long apparently possessed the quality of a 'hidden' event, and we turned to fiction in pursuit of an answer.

The quotation at the head of this chapter is taken from John Osborne's *Look Back in Anger*, the anti-Establishment play of the 1950s. In the final scene Jimmy Porter – the angry young man – discovers that his estranged wife has had a miscarriage. Alison Porter says: 'Don't you understand? It's gone! It's gone! That – that helpless human being inside my body. I thought it was so safe, and secure in there. Nothing could take it from me. It was mine, my responsibility. But it's lost. All I wanted was to die. I never knew what it was like. I didn't know it could be like that!' (Osborne, 1957).

This is one of the few literary mentions of miscarriage that exist, and it is significant that earlier in the play the tension between Alison and Jimmy erupts into this pronouncement of Jimmy's: 'Oh, my dear wife, you've got so much to learn. I only hope you learn it one day. If only something – something would happen to you, and wake you out of your beauty sleep! If you would have a child, and it would die . . . Please – if only I could watch you face that. I wonder if you might even become a recognizable human being yourself.' Hardly a pleasant request; but the implied objective, that somehow suffering the loss of a child will lead to Alison's greater maturity, is certainly a theme with echoes in some of the answers to our own questionnaire survey. Miscarriage may be the first really bad 'life event' experienced by some women, and the process of learning to accept it can be a 'growth' experience.

Since suffering is a common literary theme, we might expect a liberal use of childbearing as a topic in fiction. In the nineteenth and early twentieth centuries the most obvious consequences of women's suffering in childbearing was that they died – and there are plenty of references in Victorian novels to deaths in pregnancy or during or following childbirth. Miscarriage alone was apparently not enough to ensure the dramatic interest of the story, so that where it was mentioned, it was liable to be combined with some greater tragedy. Hence Lucretia in Hardy's *The Mayor of Casterbridge* becomes ill and miscarries, but this is merged into the recounting of her own subsequent untimely death. Similarly Fanny Robin in *Far From the Madding Crowd* succumbs in the course of a stillbirth, and Hetty Sorel in Eliot's *Adam Bede* commits infanticide. The deaths of babies were also a better illustration of suffering than miscarriage, and there must be few readers who have failed to be moved by such scenes as the death of Tess's son in Hardy's *Tess of the d'Urbervilles*:

> The baby's offence against society in coming into the world was forgotten by the girl-mother; her soul's desire was to continue that offence by preserving the life of the child.

Literary references to miscarriage are suspended in a similar air of secrecy and embarrassment as bedevils their discussion in ordinary life. Victorian prudery produced such metaphorical treatments of miscarriage as

> The Spirit fluttered for a moment on the threshold of its little prison, and unconscious of captivity, took wing (Dora's miscarriage in Dickens's *David Copperfield*, ch. XVLIII).

In Eliot's *Middlemarch* Rosamond goes riding and the horse 'took fright, and caused a worse fright to Rosamond, leading finally to the loss of her baby'. The event is referred to earlier in these terms: 'Her baby had been born prematurely, and all the embroidered robes and caps had to be laid by in darkness'.

Once we move into the twentieth century, miscarriage begins to be mentioned more openly, though by the time of A. J. Cronin's *The Citadel*, a novel by a doctor about a doctor, there is still something embarrassingly discreet about the scene in which Andrew Manson is told his wife has miscarried:

> 'Manson,' Llewellyn said gently, 'this morning – as your wife was going over the bridge – one of the rotten planks gave way. *She's* all right now, quite all right; but I'm afraid . . .'
>
> He understood even before Llewellyn finished. A great pulse of anguish beat within him.

Some of this difficulty in describing miscarriage in fiction is due to a problem recounted by women today in coming to terms with miscarriage. One of its two central characters – the fetus – lacks an identity. In novelistic terms, the reader cannot be expected to sympathize with a character who is missing from the script. In real life, mourning the death of someone you never really 'knew' is equally problematic.

Summary of themes

If it is possible briefly to summarize the main themes in a complex subject such as miscarriage, we would identify the following issues:

1. Women (and men) often feel a great need for information during and after miscarriage, and this need is not adequately met at present either by the health services or by easily available literature. To some extent the need for information must be regarded as insatiable, i.e., there are some questions, for example about why miscarriages happen, that are not likely to be answerable in the near future.

2. The need for information is not only general but personal. People want to know why miscarriage should have happened to *them*. This quest partly reflects another need often unmet, which is the need to talk through the experience of miscarriage. This is best done with someone whose own experience is relevant, either because they are involved at the level of providing medical care or because they have themselves experienced miscarriage. A common component in this working through of the experience is the tendency to blame oneself for the miscarriage. Self-blame is more likely when no clear cause for the miscarriage has been identified medically.

3. Like other loss experiences, miscarriage may be followed by a period of grieving or mourning. Sometimes the grief is suppressed in an effort towards immediate adjustment,

and also because miscarriage does not get the same social attention as the loss of a baby later in pregnancy or after birth. Thus:

4. Social attitudes to miscarriage tend to trivialize it or treat the topic with embarrassment. People feel socially inept in the face of miscarriage and so tend to deny or ignore it.

5. Miscarriage happens to women, but this does not mean that only they are affected by the reactions we have described. The fathers of the miscarried fetuses may be profoundly involved in the biological loss at an emotional level.

6. When pregnancy is unsuccessful, a key social identity, that of parenthood, is challenged. Attitudes towards miscarriage therefore cannot be understood except within the context of social values about parenthood – for both sexes.

7. Doctors – of both sexes – often do not find it emotionally easy to treat and talk to women who are having or have had miscarriages. They may be disturbed by a sense of inadequacy in medical terms – because there is little that they as doctors can do to help. It is also sometimes difficult for doctors to talk openly about life-and-death issues, since training in this sort of competence is not often part of their medical education.

8. The medical care of women during and after miscarriage may be marred both by insensitive organization of services (for example, putting gynaecological and obstetric 'cases' together in the same ward), and by poor communication with doctors and nurses.

In the closing pages of this book we comment a little further on four of these themes. These are (1) the social significance of parenthood in modern society; (2) fathers' experiences; (3) doctors' responses; and (4) practical recommendations for improving the medical care of miscarrying women.

The significance of parenthood

Miscarriages happen in both planned and unplanned pregnancies. Whether or not the pregnancy is planned, its loss may bring a feeling of failure in relation to one central adult identity for both men and women, that of parent.

Why do people want to have children? Why does not having children tend to be seen as a failure, even by those who on a rational level feel they will probably be happier without, than with, children? Despite the fall in average family size, and despite changes in the position of women which have meant a large increase in the employment of married women since the 1950s, our society is still very much oriented around parenthood as *the* status which somehow qualifies both men and women for inclusion in the adult community. In Britain the vast majority of men and women marry and become parents, at least once. This means that it may easily be regarded as deviant not to have children if one is married. Childlessness requires an explanation, whether it is voluntary or not, and this may be particularly painful for couples who want to become parents but experience miscarriage instead.

A curious feature of parenthood in our society is that it *is* somehow taken for granted. In the 'normal' course of events childhood and adolescence are succeeded by a young adulthood in which one or other heterosexual relationship leads to marriage, and marriage, after a decent interval of time, to parenthood. It is, of course, still only within marriage that having children is regarded as part of the normal train of events. In an unmarried woman pregnancy tends to be regarded as, at best, a mistake and, at worst, a disaster, as in the standard gynaecological joke:

'I've got good news for you, Mrs Brown.'
'It's Miss Brown, actually.'
'I've got bad news for you Miss Brown.'

One of the women who answered our questionnaire had miscarried a planned pregnancy while unmarried and she complained about the assumption the doctors made that she could not really want to be a mother. The way any individual woman feels about her pregnancy cannot, of course, simply be predicted from her legal status: married or not.

Within this 'taken for granted' aspect of reproduction, probably few couples seriously consider the question of whether they want children, or why they do so. Only those whose assumptions of normal parenthood are challenged by infertility or pregnancy loss are forced to confront such questions. An interesting example of this dilemma is described by the famous American anthropologist, Margaret Mead, who in her autobiography *Blackberry Winter* talks of her own experience of recurrent miscarriage and of the reasons why she became determined to achieve motherhood.

As Mead grew up, she never doubted that one day she would have a baby 'in my arms and one pulling at my skirt' (Mead, 1975). However, marriage did not bring motherhood, and she was told by doctors she would never have a child. In her second marriage she decided to accept this and bury all her commitment in work, but on visiting the harsh and aggressive New Guinea people, the Mundugumor, she realized,

> what the active refusal of children could do to a society
> . . . I felt strongly that a culture that rejected children was
> a bad culture. And so I began to hope – not very logically,
> but with a kind of emotional congruence – that perhaps
> after all I could have a child . . .

She went on to have a number of miscarriages, including one in Bali, in rather uncongenial circumstances:

> . . . I was carried up and down the muddy, steep mile from
> the main road to Bajoeng Gede. The villagers had rigged
> up a kind of sedan from one of our old bamboo chairs. But
> the bamboo had dried out, and in the middle of the trip

the chair suddenly collapsed on itself and held me as in a vice. That night, in the guesthouse in which we were staying in Kintamani, I had a rather bad miscarriage and the Dutch doctor was summoned. In those days Dutch doctors – indeed all the Dutch – strongly believed in having children. Every hotel room in the Indies had at least one crib, sometimes more. Instead of advising me not to try again for a while, the Dutch doctor said, 'You want a child, yes?' and continued with homely advice.

Mead's only live child was born, not long after, in the very different setting of a New York hospital where, according to the state law of the time, it was illegal to house mother and baby in the same room. In such a manner, cultures shape the ambition and experience of parenthood. Within this broad cultural shaping, asking *why* people want children may not make much sense. A group of women in East Anglia interviewed in one study in the 1970s expressed most of all a desire to *be mothers*, a goal for which both marriage and children were necessary. Children were also seen as essential to the survival and success of a marriage – by 'making a family' – as the source of much short-term emotional satisfaction, and as a kind of long-term investment against future loneliness. Couples who did not want children were viewed as selfish and those who could not have them were pitied.

However, as another researcher has pointed out, the selfishness ascribed to couples who do not want children is not simply the selfishness of not having chidren. Single mothers are also called selfish for their very desire to have a child of their own. Values about parenthood are intermixed with values about the family, and the belief that the family is the highest form of personal life is still widely upheld in Britain today.

Yet whatever one believes about the family, bearing a child is the unique achievement of women. A commitment to sex equality, the equal rights of women inside and outside the home, and so forth, does not necessitate a childless identity nor free one from the agonizing dilemma of whether, or how, to become a mother. In a book called *Why Children?*, the eighteen women who publicly air their most private decisions about, and encounters with, motherhood make three facts abundantly plain. Firstly, the possibility of childbearing is something that women can scarcely ever dismiss with ease. Even with a firm commitment to a childless state, even with six children, even with a stark diagnosis of infertility, the potential for motherhood is somehow always inside not only women's bodies but their psychologies too. Secondly, parenthood is a double-edged sword. Each child brings both pain and joy. Thirdly, the idea of 'choice' here is to some extent a red herring. In a society still so strongly engaged with the ideology and practice of family life, and with a continuing view of women as mothers, the notion that any of us is completely free to choose what we do is, at least, idealistic, and, at worst, deceptive.

This, then, is the general background against which women and men experience, and adjust to, miscarriage. It is only in this light that some couples' reactions to miscarriage make sense, for the inability to complete pregnancy may profoundly disturb a set of values believed in so entirely that one is not even aware of them.

The absent father

Fathers are not conspicuously present in our book. Although we did set out to include them in the more obvious places, we faced the usual difficulty that much of the medical and sociological research on miscarriage and parenthood has ignored fathers. For instance, the male biological contribution to miscarriage has received very much less attention in medical research than the female contribution. There is, so far as we know, no study of fathers' responses to miscarriage. Our own questionnaire was filled in by women – though the husband's role in supporting his wife through the experience of miscarriage was quite often commented on, so that husbands emerged top of the league table of 'helpful people' quoted in chapter 4. A typical answer to the question 'Who was most helpful to you?' ran as follows: 'My husband. He was absolutely marvellous. He just let me get it out of my system without telling me to pull myself together.' (Margaret Dwyer).

We quoted some husbands' responses to their wives' miscarriages at the end of chapter 5. One husband appended to the questionnaire completed by his wife the following comments comparing her first and second pregnancies – it was the second which ended in miscarriage:

I noticed a great difference in my wife's behaviour between the beginning of the first pregnancy and the second. It may of course just be due to our change of circumstances. In the first pregnancy my wife seemed calmer (although it was a new experience). She worked as a secretary right up until she was seven and a half months. We lived in a flat at the time . . . so there wasn't a lot of housework. During the second pregnancy, even before her pregnancy had been confirmed, she seemed very tense, nervous, short-tempered, very emotional and generally seemed on edge. It may have been a change in her hormonal balance that was telling us something was wrong . . . There certainly wasn't any such change in her during her first pregnancy. (Eric Murray)

Many men are highly involved in their partners' pregnancies and very sensitive to any psychological or physical changes. But, at the same time, it is probably true that men have a different kind of investment in parenthood from women, and therefore their reactions to miscarriage may also be different. In one study of men's responses to infertility, men talked not only about their own desire to have children, but their desire to provide their partners with the status and role of mother. Having a child was seen as intrinsically fulfilling for a woman and as providing some sort of career for her. The men's major adult identity was vested in their work, and although it was important to *become* a father, making it possible for the woman to *be* a mother came first. What this means, of course, is that if a man feels he is somehow responsible for his partner's failure to have children, then he is likely to consider he has let her down in a very fundamental way.

The other main difficulty encountered by men whose partners miscarry is probably that of being able to allow themselves to express their emotions at all adequately. Social expectations of men's behaviour in such situations are that men will be strong and not give way to feelings of weakness and vulnerability. The woman may break down, but it is the man's duty to support her. For this reason, some men may find themselves having the kind of 'delayed' reaction to their partners' miscarriage described by Dorothy Alexander in chapter 5. It may also happen that if a woman continues to mourn the lost fetus for an unusually long time, her partner may become impatient with her lengthy emotional dependence on him. This has been found to be the case sometimes after stillbirth. The chances of these difficulties occurring are less if the partners talk freely to one another. But while this advice is easy to hand out, it is much more difficult to follow in the perturbed period following the unexpected loss of a pregnancy.

Medical attitudes

Some of what we have said about fathers also applies to doctors too. An article in the medical journal the *Lancet* in 1977 called the occurrence of 'death in utero . . . extraordinarily chilling and repugnant', and went on to note the emotional inability of many doctors to come to terms with pregnancy loss in their patients. The article was dealing specifically with stillbirth but miscarriage is another point on the spectrum of pregnancy loss, so some of the same points are likely to apply to miscarriage too.

Another study carried out some years before, and quoted in the *Lancet* article, observed, on the basis of doctors' responses to a questionnaire about stillbirth, that they 'are completely reluctant to know, notice, or remember anything about these patients'. Sometimes a doctor may feel he or she should not get emotionally involved with patients, since this is not in the patient's best interests. This is often because the doctor is actually also protecting himself or herself from the anguish of a disturbing encounter with a distressed patient. Doctors are not exempt from feelings that they have not been able to do whatever is required. The same is true of midwives and nurses, where their reactions have been studied. When midwives, nurses or doctors will have experienced pregnancy loss themselves, a different basis potentially exists for sympathizing with the woman and her partner: this may make communication and support easier.

Several doctors we talked to told us about how distressing they personally found it to be responsible for the medical care of a woman who was miscarrying. One doctor, now no longer involved in clinical work, gave us the following story:

In 1972–3 I was working on a gynaecological ward where late abortions were done. In the same ward there was a woman with a history of midtrimester miscarriage who came in for a shirodkar suture at fourteen weeks. She stayed in hospital until twenty-two weeks, when she went into labour. I had to take her suture out, and I remember having to fight to see through my tears in order to do it. I found it very hard being expected to cope with the contradiction of some women not being able to hang on to wanted pregnancies, and others needing to have terminations of pregnancies with which they feel they can't continue. A medical training doesn't necessarily equip one to deal with the emotional aspects of pregnancy loss.

It was notable, among responses to our questionnaire,

that those occasions when a doctor or nurse did talk openly and supportively with a woman about her miscarriage, and did express an attitude of involvement and caring, were always very much appreciated.

To supplement the information we had about patients' attitudes, we carried out a small survey of 20 GPs and 5 consultant obstetricians in one area health authority to find out how they treated women who were threatening to miscarry or who had miscarried. We did not ask directly about how the doctor felt emotionally in such situations, but what was notable in many of their replies was the overriding desire to be able to do or offer something. This is perhaps one factor behind the variation in treatments advised by different doctors.

Both among the GPs and among the consultants, there was great variation in treatments suggested and advice given. For example, when the GPs were asked, 'What advice do you give to women with slight bleeding in early pregnancy?', there was a scatter of answers, with 40 per cent telling patients to go to bed and 40 per cent advising normal behaviour. Among the five consultants, two said, 'go to bed', one said, 'behave as usual but don't move house', one replied, 'behave as usual but stop having intercourse', and one advised injections of HCG. Other areas where there was disagreement among the GPs was in who should have ultrasound, who should be referred for genetic counselling, whether 'the products of conception' should be sent for analysis, when women should return to paid work and how soon a woman should try to conceive again.

About other aspects of treatment, there was more consensus. Not surprisingly, most GPs (65 per cent) saw heavy bleeding as an indicator for referral to hospital, and 95 per cent saw heavy bleeding associated with pain as an indicator for hospital referral. There was also consensus on which women needed a D & C, with 90 per cent of GPs seeing continued bleeding as an appropriate reason. The consultants showed a marked difference from the GPs in their attitudes to D & C. They felt that following almost all

195

early miscarriages a D & C was necessary, whereas only 10 per cent of GPs would take this view. These differences obviously reflect the different experiences of GPs and consultants.

Most GPs and consultants did not feel it necessary to give advice about whether or not to bathe or use tampons after miscarriage, but they did give advice on when to conceive again, when to resume intercourse, contraception and paid work, although here again the advice was not always consistent. Perhaps it is interesting to note that the only time there was a difference between the male and female GPs questioned (there were no female consultants) was with regard to the use of tampons – with women tending to give advice on this, while the men did not.

The consultants usually did not mention the possibility that there may be psychological effects following a miscarriage. Four out of five said this was because after a miscarriage they usually did not see the woman on the wards. Women were, however, seen by junior staff and nurses before discharge, and the consultants hoped the psychological aspect was discussed by these professionals. Only one consultant said he thought it wrong to bring up the possibility of psychological problems, as he felt 'such ideas should not be introduced as most people had enough problems to deal with and it was wrong to increase people's anxiety in this way'. Eighty-five per cent of the GPs discussed the likelihood of some psychological aftermath. What they said usually covered possible feelings of guilt, loss and bereavement, and several GPs did mention that they would not only *say* something to women in this situation, but would try to listen carefully to what the women themselves had to say.

Practical suggestions

We come finally to some of the suggestions for improving the treatment of couples experiencing miscarriage made by the women in our survey, or arising in some way from our research in this area. Top of the list we would put:

1. The need for discussion with medical staff and for emotional support. Perhaps women should articulate this need as much as the providers of care should be expected to respond sensitively to it. To say, 'I need to talk about what happened: will you let me talk, and tell me what you know?' isn't easy, but the trap of not discussing difficult events such as miscarriage is one in which we are all caught. It seems particularly important that medical staff do not 'de-personalize' the event by talking in abstract medical language. As one woman wrote,

> I'm glad the medical profession is beginning to emphasize the emotional side of miscarriage. Everyone talked about my 'pregnancy' or 'the fetus' but to me it was my baby. Also they don't realize how guilty you can feel – it may be irrational but I felt my babies died because I had failed to keep them alive. It's a very difficult thing to talk about when you are all emotional and confused, but I think it's something that needs to be acknowledged and brought out into the open so that the woman can learn to cope.

Fiona Hoffman's experience of going to hospital for a D & C after her miscarriage was recounted by a number of women:

> In 24 hours I saw the nurse who gave me the pre-med, the porter who took me to theatre, the anaesthetist, the

nurse who gave me my post-op wash and the doctor who discharged me. No one gave me any form of counselling . . . I feel very strongly that there should be counselling after a miscarriage and plenty of support through subsequent pregnancies. Also, a great improvement in the attitude of nurses and doctors when dealing with a woman who is threatening to miscarry. It might have been a frog-like fetus to them, but to my husband and I it was our first child.

Other women simply noted this point as, for example, 'need for a meeting with consultant or GP *very soon after the event*, for advice and information'. Others suggested more specific forms of counselling for women after miscarriage:

I think there is a real need for support or counselling after a miscarriage. My two were fairly early but still traumatic, I'm sure one at 20–24 weeks must be devastating.

As someone else pointed out, 'They have counselling for divorced people, also widows, so why not when you have a miscarriage?'

This counselling should include husbands, as another woman noted:

I also feel that husbands should be counselled better. This is the only fault I can find with the first hospital. The husband seems to be forgotten. It's hard to explain to them what went wrong when you are not sure yourself.

What is *not* necessarily needed, as Susan Watson says, is a prescription for anti-depressants:

I went to my doctor a week after I was discharged from

hospital to get a tonic as I was feeling very tired and listless, and the first thing he offered me was tablets for depression. I did not take them from him as I felt I did not need them. I know some people do but I feel he was wrong to offer them so easily when a chat about the miscarriage may be all the person needs to talk over their anxiety.

A 'helpline' was one other recommendation, and, of course, the help provided by miscarriage support groups is precisely of this kind:

> I think it would be marvellous if there was some kind of 'helpline' set up for people who've had a miscarriage, because I felt like a freak when it happened to me. I think it hit me particularly hard as after 20 weeks I thought I was 'home and dry'; if it had been in the first 12 weeks as it usually is, I may have been able to accept that there was a possibility of something being wrong with the baby. Whereas I was told that there was nothing wrong with mine.

> Miscarriage support groups [MSG] need to be encouraged. To suffer in isolation (as I did) is heartbreaking. Since MSG set up in this area, I have found I am not unique. Others have lost as many babies, many have gone on to produce babies (gives encouragement). Can talk about miscarriage freely, expressing emotions and anxieties. No longer feel a freak! Have made new friends! Many of us are far from our families and will need support for future pregnancies. MSG will provide this.

2. A number of women noted a lack of coordination between GP, hospital and community medical services which meant that the question of who was responsible for the aftercare of miscarrying women was never asked, let alone answered:

I think they should send someone round to see you from the hospital (if you go). Like they do when the health visitor comes when you have your baby.

After I was discharged from hospital and came home, that was it, all the help stopped and I was left to get over it by myself. I think it would have helped me if I could have talked to someone who knew how I was feeling. Everyone seemed afraid to talk to me, let alone about what had happened.

There seems to be a lack of coordination between GP and hospital. After my second miscarriage I was very depressed and wanted to discuss what had happened in medical terms. Hospital discharged me with no comment except 'see your GP in 2 weeks'. GP examined me – no comment.

3. A complaint which has been made for many years also surfaced in our survey. In some hospitals women who are losing, or have lost, their pregnancies are put in the same ward as newly delivered mothers and their babies, or as those awaiting termination of pregnancy. This can be distressing to all concerned, and should clearly be avoided where possible:

I have one thing against the hospital I stayed in. They put my bed next to a girl who was waiting for abortion, which made things worse for me. I think they should put us in different wards.

With a growing sensitivity among health-care professionals to the social and emotional side of both successful and unsuccessful childbearing, it is to be hoped that these recommendations will come into effect.

New research may enlighten us about the causes of miscarriage, and it may also be that effective and safe new forms of treatment are found in the future to prevent it. But some miscarriages will still happen, and some couples will continue to find the pathway to parenthood more hazardous than others. It is only human to regard the experience of miscarriage seriously as an event that requires explanation and support. It is a mark of a humane society to meet the needs of those couples who lose their babies, just as it is to help towards happy parenthood those who do not.

Appendix I: The Survey

One of the symptoms of the relative lack of research on the subject of miscarriage is absence of information about women's experiences of miscarriage. We became aware of this when we started to write this book, and felt a need throughout to refer to women's experiences. However, we were not in a position (at that stage) to carry out our own research. What we decided to do as very much a second best was to send out some questionnaires to women willing to tell us something about their miscarriage experiences. The questionnaires asked for a few personal details (the woman's age and occupation and her partner's occupation) and asked a number of questions about each miscarriage a woman had had: when it happened, what the symptoms were, whether a doctor was contacted, whether the woman went into hospital and had a D and C. We also enquired about the information and advice a woman had received, what she thought of her medical treatment, whether she had any idea as to what had caused the miscarriage, and how she felt, physically and emotionally, afterwards.

In order to find women willing to give us this information we asked the editors of *Mother and Baby* magazine and of the newsletter of the National Association for the Childless to publish our request for help: they kindly agreed to do so. In addition, members of a miscarriage support group filled in some questionnaires, and we received other accounts from women who heard that we were interested in learning about women's experiences of miscarriage. The result of all this was 137 completed questionnaires describing a total of 219 miscarriages. It is these questionnaires that we have drawn on throughout this book.

Appendix I: The Survey

There is nothing magic or necessarily representative about the 137 completed questionnaires. We could have ended up with many more, but felt that this number was about all we could handle. (We would like to apologize to those women who wrote in asking for a questionnaire, only to get the response that we had sent out enough: it wasn't that we weren't interested in *their* experiences.) We are very aware that our 137 do not constitute a random sample. We do not know whether or not the women who wrote to us are representative of all women having miscarriages in Britain. Of course there are good reasons to suspect that they aren't typical, for they needed to be sufficiently affected by their miscarriages to want to tell us about them. It is also likely that women dissatisfied with their medical care are over-represented among the women who filled in our questionnaires. As we've said, it is well-known that satisfied patients are less likely than dissatisfied patients to air their opinions. Furthermore, questionnaire surveys such as this normally do not tap the experiences of all social groups within the population equally. Those who are comfortable with form-filling and expressing their personal experiences in writing are more likely to complete a questionnaire.

Having said all that, we thought it would be a good idea to supply some basic details about our questionnaire sample. For example, their age: the average age of all the women taken together was 27 years 10 months, with the women who belonged to the National Association for the Childless and the miscarriage support group being, on average, rather older than the readers of *Mother and Baby*. As to their occupations, it's difficult to be terribly informative since only 117 stated an occupation on the questionnaire and, of those, 76 simply wrote 'housewife'. Table 9.1 gives the information we do have about the women's and their partner's occupations.

Table 9.1 **The occupations of questionnaire respondents**

	Mother %	Father %
Housewife	65	0
Manual (e.g., welder)	2	35
Non-manual (e.g., clerk)	21	39
Professional (e.g., solicitor)	12	23
Unemployed	0	3
Total stating an occupation	100	100

As one would expect, the percentage of people with manual occupations is considerably lower in this sample than in the population as a whole, and the percentage with professional occupations is higher.

Not all the women who filled in the questionnaires told us how many weeks pregnant they had been when they miscarried. Of the 136 miscarriages that were 'dated' in this way, the timing was distributed as shown in table 9.2.

Table 9.2 **Stage of pregnancy at which miscarriages among questionnaire respondents occurred**

	% miscarriages for which this information given
6–12 weeks	62
13–15 weeks	12
16–20 weeks	14
21–28 weeks	12
Total	100

Nearly two-thirds were early miscarriages, in the first twelve weeks of pregnancy, and only about one in ten happened after twenty weeks.

Appendix II: Resources

Groups

Many women told us that they had found it helpful to talk to other women about their experience of miscarriage. There is a miscarriage association and several miscarriage support groups in various parts of the country. The aims of the Miscarriage Association are to provide support, help and information for women and their families who have had, or are having, miscarriages, and feel the need for help. If you write to the women at the Miscarriage Association, they may be able to put you in touch with a local group. Their address is:

Dolphin Cottage
4 Ashfield Terrace
Thorpe
Near Wakefield
West Yorkshire WF12 9QH

In some areas, local groups of the National Childbirth Trust provide support for women who have had miscarriages, and they have produced a booklet on miscarriage which can be obtained from:

The National Childbirth Trust
5 Queensborough Terrace
London W2 3TB
Tel: 01-221 3833

If you have any difficulty in conceiving, or in maintaining a pregnancy, the National Association for the Childless provides information and support, and is also involved in research. Their address is:

318 Summer Lane
Birmingham B19 3RL
Tel: Birmingham (021) 359 4887

A helpful book, written by two women who have experienced infertility, is *The Experience of Infertility* by Naomi Pfeffer and Anne Woollett (Virago, 1983).

Before conceiving and in early pregnancy
The Maternity Alliance has a booklet on preconceptional care. Their address is:

309 Kentish Town Road
London NW5 2TJ
Tel: 01-267 3255

Diet
Barbara Pickard has written two booklets about diet before and during pregnancy: *Are You Fit Enough to Become Pregnant?* and *Nausea and Vomiting in Early Pregnancy.* These are both available from her at 80 pence a copy plus large s.a.e. Her address is:

Barbara Pickard
Lane End Farm
Denton
Ilkley
West Yorkshire LS29 0HP
Tel: Ilkley (0943) 609209

Medical care
There are a number of organizations which can give information, support and advice about how to find sympathetic medical care in pregnancy, and which are interested in how to improve maternity care in general.

These organizations include the NCT (address above) and also the Association for Improvements in the Maternity Services (AIMS):

Christine Rodgers
163 Liverpool Road
London N1 0RF
Tel: 01-378 5628

References

Introduction

Granville, A. B. (1819): *a report of the practice of midwifery at the Westminster General Dispensary during 1818.* London, Burgess and Hill.

Chapter 1

Hassold, T., Quillen, S. D. and Yamane, J. A. (1983): 'Sex ratio in spontaneous abortions'. *Ann. Hum. Genet.*, 47, 39–47.

Hertig, A. T. and Rock, J. (1949): 'A series of potentially abortive ova recovered from fertile women prior to the first missed menstrual period'. *Am. J. Obs. and Gynecol.* 58(5), 968–93.

Macfarlane, A. and Mugford, M. (1984): *Birth Counts: Statistics of Pregnancy and Childbirth.* London, HMSO.

Miller, J. F., Williamson, E., Glue, J., *et al.* (1980): 'Fetal loss after implantation'. *Lancet*, 13 September, 554–6.

Porter, I. H., and Hook, E. B. (1980): *Human Embryonic and Fetal Death.* New York, Academic Press.

Roberts, C. J. and Lowe, C. R. (1975): 'Where have all the conceptions gone?' *Lancet*, 1 March, 498–9.

Rushton, D. I. (1978): 'Simplified classification of spontaneous abortions'. *J. Med. Genet.*, 15, 1–9.

Weathersbee, P. S. (1980): 'Early reproductive loss and the factors that may influence its occurrence'. *J. Repr. Med.*, 25, 315–18.

Whittaker, P. G., Taylor, A. and Lind, T. (1983): 'Unsuspected pregnancy loss in healthy women'. *Lancet*, 21 May, 1126–7.

Chapter 2

Hemminki, K., Niemi, M.-L., Saloniemi, I., *et al.* (1980): 'Spontaneous abortions by occupation and social class in Finland'. *Int. J. Epidemiol.* 9(2), 149–53.

Hemminki, K., Sorsa, M. and Vainio, H. (1979): 'Genetic risks

References

caused by occupational chemicals'. *Scand. J. Work Environ. and Hlth*, 5, 307–27.

Leifer, M. (1980): *Psychological Effects of Motherhood*. New York, Praeger.

Oakley, A. (1981): *From Here to Maternity*. Harmondsworth, Penguin.

Chapter 3

Alberman, E., Creasy, M., Elliott, M. and Spicer, C. (1976): 'Maternal factors associated with fetal chromosomal anomalies in spontaneous abortions'. *Br. J. Obstet. and Gynaecol.*, 83, 621–7.

Alberman, E., Polani, P. E., Fraser Roberts, J. A. *et al.* (1972): 'Parental X-irradiation and chromosome constitution in their spontaneously aborted foetuses'. *Ann. Hum. Genet.*, London, 36, 185–94.

Axelsson, G., and Rylander, R. (1982): 'Exposure to anaesthetic gases and spontaneous abortion: response bias in a postal questionnaire study'. *Int. J. Epidemiol.* 11 (3), 250–6.

Blondel, J. (1729): *The Power of the Mother's Imagination Over the Foetus Exam'd*. London.

British Medical Journal editorial (1978): 'Cigarette smoking and spontaneous abortion'. *Br. Med. J.*, 3 February, 6108, 259

Chamberlain, G., and Garcia, J. (1983): 'Prematurity and occupational activity during pregnancy'. Unpublished paper, INSERM, Paris, France.

Crane, J. P. (1981): 'The role of maternal diabetes in repetitive spontaneous abortion'. *Fertility and Sterility*, 36 (4), 477–9.

Dobbs, J. and Marsh, A. (1983): 'Smoking among secondary school children'. OPCS, Social Survey Division, London, HMSO.

Guerrero, R. V. and Rojas, O. I. (1975): 'Spontaneous abortion and aging of human ova and spermatozoa'. *New Engl. J. Med.* 293, 573–5.

Harlap, S. and Shiono, P. H. (1980): 'Alcohol, smoking, and incidence of spontaneous abortions in the first and second trimester'. *Lancet*, 26 July, 173–6.

Harlap, S., Shiono, P. H., Ramcharan, S., *et al.* (1979): 'A prospective study of spontaneous fetal losses after induced abortions'. *New Engl. J. Med.* 301 (13), 677-81.

Harlap, S., Shiono, P. H. and Ramcharan, S. (1980): 'Spontaneous fetal losses in women using different contraceptives around the time of conception'. *Int. J. Epidemiol.* 9(1), 49-56.

Hellman, L. M., Duffus, G. M., Donald, I. and Sunden, B. (1970): 'Safety of diagnostic ultrasound in obstetrics'. *Lancet*, 30 May, 1133–4.

Hemminki, K., Mutanen, P., Saloniemi, I., *et al.* (1982): 'Spontaneous abortions in hospital staff engaged in sterilizing instruments with chemical agents'. *Br. Med. J.* 285, 1461–3.

Himes, N. E. (1963): *Medical History of Contraception*. New York, Gamut Press.

Jouppila, P. (1980): 'Clinical and ultrasonic aspects in the diagnosis and follow-up of patients with early pregnancy failure'. *Acta Obstet. Gynecol. Scand.* 59, 405–9.

Keirse, M. J. N. C., Rush, R. W., Anderson, A. B. M. and Turnbull, A. C. (1978): 'Risk of pre-term delivery in patients with previous pre-term delivery and/or abortion'. *Br. J. Obstet. Gynaecol.*, 15, 81–5.

Kinlen, L. J. and Acheson, E. D. (1968): 'Diagnostic irradiation, congenital malformations and spontaneous abortion'. *Br. J. Radiol.*, 41, 648–54.

Kline, J., Stein, Z. A., Susser, M. and Warburton, D. (1977): 'Smoking: a risk factor for spontaneous abortion'. *New Engl. J. Med.*, 297, 793–6.

Kline, J., Stein, Z. A., Susser, M. and Warburton, D. (1977): 'Spontaneous abortion and the use of sugar substitutes (saccharin)'. *Am. J. Obstet. Gynecol.*, 130, 708–11.

Kline, J., Stein, Z., Shrout, P. *et al.* (1980): 'Drinking during pregnancy and spontaneous abortion'. *Lancet*, 26 July, 176–80.

Lancet editorial (1980): 'Alcohol and spontaneous abortion'. *Lancet*, 26 July, 188.

Lancet editorial (1983): 'Maternal blocking antibodies, the fetal allograft and recurrent abortion'. *Lancet*, 19 November, 1175–6.

Livingston, J. E. and Poland, B. J. (1980): 'A study of spontaneously aborted twins'. *Teratology*, 21, 139–48.

Mamelle, N., Laumon, B. and Lazar, P. (1983): 'Prematurity and occupational activity during pregnancy'. Unpublished paper, INSERM, Paris, France.

Oakley, A., Macfarlane, A. and Chalmers, I. (1982): 'Social class, stress and reproduction' in A. R. Rees and H. Purcell (eds.), *Disease and the Environment*. Chichester, John Wiley.

References

Poland, B. J., Miller, J. R., Harris, M. and Livingston, J. (1981): 'Spontaneous abortion: a study of 1,961 women and their conceptuses'. *Acta Obstet. Gynecol. Scand. Suppl.*, 102.

Porter, I. H. and Hook, E. B. (1980): *Human Embryonic and Fetal Death*. New York, Academic Press.

Redman, C. W. G. (1983): 'Immune factors and recurrent abortion: a review'. *Personal Communication*.

Rush, D. (1982): 'Effects of changes in protein and calorie intake during pregnancy on the growth of the human fetus' in M. Enkin and I. Chalmers (eds.), *Effectiveness and Satisfaction in Antenatal Care*. London, Spastics International Medical Publications and William Heinemann Medical Books.

Schoenbaum, S. C., Monson, R. R., Stubblefield, P. G., *et al.* (1980): 'Outcome of the delivery following an induced or spontaneous abortion'. *Am. J. Obstet. Gynecol.*, 136, 19–23.

Stewart, A., Webb, J. and Hewitt, D. (1958): 'A survey of childhood malignancies'. *Br. Med. J.*, 28 June, 1495–1508.

Strobino, B. R., Kline, J. and Stein, Z. (1978): 'Chemical and physical exposures of parents: effects on human reproduction and offspring'. *Early Human Development*, 1/4, 371–99.

Tatum, H. J., Schmidt, F. H. and Jain, A. K. (1976): 'Management and outcome of pregnancies associated with the Copper T intrauterine contraceptive device'. *Am. J. Obstet, Gynecol.*, 126, 869–79.

Taylor, C. and Page Faulk, W. (1981): 'Prevention of recurrent abortion with leucocyte transfusions'. *Lancet*, 11 July, 68–9.

Vessey, M. P., Johnson, B., Doll, R. and Peto, R. (1974): 'Outcome of pregnancy in women using an intrauterine device'. *Lancet*, 23 March, 495–8.

Vessey, M., Meisler, L., Flavel, R. and Yeates, D. (1979): 'Outcome of pregnancy in women using different methods of contraception'. *Br. J. Obstet. Gynaecol.*, 86, 548–56.

Warburton, D., Susser, M., Stein, Z. and Kline, J. (1979): 'Genetic and epidemiologic investigation of spontaneous abortion: relevance to clinical practice'. *Birth Defects: Original Article Series*, vol. XV, No. 5, 127–36.

Warner, R. H. and Rosett, H. L. (1975) 'The effects of drinking on offspring. An historical survey of the American and British literature'. *J. Studies on Alcohol*, 36 (11), 1395–420.

Chapter 4

British Medical Journal editorial (1980): 'Vaginal bleeding in early pregnancy'. *Br. Med. J.*, 16 August, 470.

Chamberlain, G., Philipp, E., Howlett, B. and Masters, K. (1978): *British Births 1970.* London, William Heinemann Medical Books.

Funderburk, S. J., Guthrie, D. and Meldrum, D. (1980): 'Outcome of pregnancies complicated by early vaginal bleeding'. *Br. J. Obstet. Gynaecol.* 87, 100–5.

Heinonen, O. P. (1977): 'Birth defects and drugs in pregnancy' *Collaborative Perinatal Project*

Johannsen, A. (1970): 'The prognosis of threatened abortion'. *Acta Obstet. Gynecol. Scand.*, 49, 89–93.

Chapter 5

Badinter, E. (1981): *The Myth of Motherhood.* London, Souvenir Press.

Gordon, L. (1977): *Woman's Body, Woman's Right.* Harmondsworth, Penguin.

Granville, A. B. (1819): *A report of the practice of midwifery at the Westminster General Dispensary during 1818.* London, Burgess and Hill.

Hall, R. (1978): *Dear Dr Stopes.* Harmondsworth, Penguin.

Llewellyn Davies, M. (ed.) (1915, reprinted 1978): *Maternity: Letters from Working Women.* London, Virago.

McFalls, J. A. Jr (1968): 'Psychic stress and pregnancy loss' in Tupper and Weil, *Psychopathology and Subfecundity*, p. 757.

Mead, M. and Newton, N. (1967): 'Cultural patterning of perinatal behaviour' in Richardson, S. A., and Guttmacher, A. F. (eds.), *Childbearing - Its Social and Psychological Aspects.* Baltimore, Williams and Williams.

Seibel, M. and Graves, W. L. (1980): 'The psychological implications of spontaneous abortions'. *J. Repr. Med.* 25, 161–5.

Chapter 6

Beral, V. (1975): 'An epidemiological study of recent trends in ectopic pregnancy'. *Br. J. Obstet. Gynaecol.*, 82, 775–82.

British Medical Journal editorial (1980): 'Unanswered questions on ectopic pregnancy'. *Br. Med. J.*, 3 May, 1127–8.

References

Erkkola, R. and Liukko, P. (1977): 'Intrauterine device and ectopic pregnancy'. *Contraception*, 16, 569–74.

Hlavin, G. E., Ladocsi, L. T. and Breen, J. L. (1978): 'Ectopic pregnancy: an analysis of 153 patients'. *Int. J. Gynecol. Obstet.* 16, 42–7.

Robinson, N. and Beral, V. (1979): 'Risk of ectopic pregnancy'. *Lancet*, 8 December, 1247.

Scott, J. S., Lynch, E. M. and Anderson, J. A. (1976): 'Surgical treatment of female infertility: value of paradoxical oophorectomy'. *Br. Med. J.*, 13 March, 631–4.

Sivin, L. (1979): 'Copper T IUD use and ectopic rates in the United States'. *Contraception*, 19, 151–73.

Westrom, I., Bengtsson, L. P. and Mardh, P. A. (1981): 'Incidence, trends and risks of ectopic pregnancy in a population of women'. *Br. Med. J.*, 3 January, 15-18.

Chapter 7

Anderson, A. (1983): 'Evaluation of Treatment'. *Personal Communication*.

Anderson, A. and Turnbull, A. C. (1982): 'Effect of oestrogens, progestogens and betamimetics in pregnancy' in Enkin, M. and Chalmers, I. (eds.), *Effectiveness and Satisfaction in Antenatal Care*. London, Spastics International Medical Publications & William Heinemann Medical Books, pp. 163–181.

Chamberlain, G., (1982): 'Recurrent miscarriage and preterm labour' in Harley, J. M. G. (ed.), *Clinics in Obstetrics and Gynaecology*, vol. 9, no. 1, pp. 115–30. London, W. B. Saunders.

Diddle, A. W., O'Connor, K. A., Jack, R. and Pearse, R. I. (1953): 'Evaluation of bedrest in threatened abortion'. *Obstet. and Gynecol.* 2 (1), 63–7.

Chapter 8

Erickson, J. D. and Bjerkedal, T. (1978): 'Interpregnancy interval: association with birth weight, stillbirth, and neonatal death'. *J. Epid. Comm. Hlth*, 32, 124–30.

Fedrick, J. and Adelstein, P. (1973): 'Influence of pregnancy spacing on outcome of pregnancy'. *Br. Med. J.*, 4, 753–6.

Glass, R. and Golbus, M. S. (1978): 'Habitual abortion'. *Fertility and Sterility*, 29 (3), 257–65.

Heritage, D. W., English, S. C., Young, R. B. and Chen, A. T. L. (1978): 'Cytogenetics of recurrent abortions'. *Fertility and Sterility*, 29 (4), 414–16.

Hertig, A. T. and Livingstone, R. G. (1944): 'Spontaneous, threatened and habitual abortion: their pathogenesis and treatment'. *New Engl. J. Med.* 230 (26), 797–806.

Lumley, J. (1982): 'Advice in pregnancy: perfect remedies, imperfect science' in Enkin, E. and Chalmers, I. (eds.), *Effectiveness and Satisfaction in Antenatal Care*. London, Spastics International Medical Publications & William Heinemann Medical Books, pp. 132–50.

Poland, B. J., Miller, J. R., Jones, D. C. and Trimble, B. K. (1977): 'Reproductive counselling in patients who have had a spontaneous abortion'. *Am. J. Obstet. Gynecol.* 127 (7), 685–91.

Sant-Cassia, L. J. and Cooke, P. (1981): 'Chromosomal analysis of couples with repeated spontaneous abortions'. *Br. J. Obster. Gynaecol.* 88, 52–8.

Stenchever, M. A., Parks, K. J., Daines, T. L., *et al.* (1977): 'Cytogenetics of habitual abortion and other reproductive wastage'. *Am. J. Obstet. Gynecol.* 127, 143–50.

Chapter 9

Bourne, S. (1971): 'The psychological effects of stillbirths on the doctor' in *Psychosomatic Medicine in Obstetrics and Gynaecology*, 3rd International Congress. Karger, London, pp. 333–4.

Busfield, J. and Paddon, M. (1977): *Thinking About Children*. Cambridge University Press.

Cronin, A. J. (1965): *The Citadel*. London, Four Square Books (first published 1937).

Dickens, C. (1849): *David Copperfield*.

Dowrick, S. and Grundberg, S. (1980): *Why Children?* London, The Women's Press.

Eliot, G. (1965): *Middlemarch*. Harmondsworth, Penguin (first published 1871–2).

Eliot, G. (1859): *Adam Bede*

Hardy, T. (1975): *Far From the Madding Crowd*. London, Macmillan (first published 1874).

Hardy, T. (1978): *The Mayor of Casterbridge*. Harmondsworth, Penguin (first published 1886).

References

Hardy, T. (1975): *Tess of the d'Urbervilles*. London, Macmillan (first published 1891).

Lancet editorial (1977): 'The abhorrence of stillbirth'. *Lancet*, 4 June, 1188–90.

Mead, M. (1975): *Blackberry Winter*. New York, Pocket Books.

Osborne, J. (1957): *Look Back in Anger*. London, Faber and Faber.

Owens, D. (1982): 'The desire to father: reproductive ideologies and involuntarily childless men' in McKee, L. and O'Brien, M. (eds.), *The Father Figure*. London, Tavistock.

Stringham, J. G., Riley, J. H. and Ross, A. (1982): 'Silent birth: mourning a stillborn baby'. *Social Work*, July, 322–7.

Index

Index

Index

medical staff
    attitudes of (to miscarriage) 98–101, 194–7
medication *see* drugs
meiosis 54
membranes
    rupture of 34, 85
menstrual cycle 39, 43, 49, 50, 65, 78, 140
menstruation 43; *see also* periods
Mersiline Tape 154
Middlemarch 185
midwife 84, 180, 194
miscarriage
    accounts of 12, 20–4 *passim*, 29–36 *passim*, 84–101 *passim*, 103–14 *passim*, 119, 125–6, 133–43 *passim*, 148, 155, 156, 160–5 *passim*, 170–6 *passim*, 190
    adjustment to 35–6, 102, 132
    causes of 17, 40, 58–82, 114–19
    chances of successful pregnancy following 17, 160–81 *passim*
    children's reactions to 23, 99
    cultural attitudes to 118–22
    definition of 18, 21, 26–7
    emotional response to 13, 17, 29
    experiences of 17, 18, 83–101
    historical data 13, 117, 119–21
    hospitalization and 39, 90, 196
    incidence of 12, 15, 16, 183
    in literature 182–6 *passim*
    medical management of 24
    paternal factors in 58, 66–7, 77–8, 116
    rates of 73–4, 77, 78
    research on (lack of) 91, 158, 201, 203
    studies of 13, 16, 39, 133, 146
    symptoms of 19, 83–9
    treatment of 17, 144–59, 195–7
Miscarriage Association 207
miscarriage support group 199, 203, 207
mitosis 54
mongolism *see* Down's syndrome

monosomy 60, 61
morning sickness 179; *see also* nausea
Mother and Baby 12, 203
mourning 122–8, 193
Mugford, M. *see* Macfarlane, A.

National Association for the Childless 12, 177, 203, 207–8
National Childbirth Trust 33, 207
nausea 19, 20, 55, 83, 87, 136
neural crest 62
New Guinea 189
nightmares *see* dreams
nurse 99, 194

Oakley, A. 55
occupation 58, 73–4
oestradiol 43, 49
oestrogen 41, 43, 50, 130, 145, 147
'old wives tales' 55
orgasm 71
Osborne, John 182, 184
ovary 41, 43, 49, 52, 54
'overdoing it' 114, 115
ovulation 43, 49, 50
ovum 41, 42, 43, 49; *see also* blighted ovum
Owens, David 193

pain 19, 83–4, 136–7
    in shoulder 137–8
paracetamol 79
parenthood
    significance of 188–92
partner 99, 116, 126–7, 192–3
penicillin 79
perinatal mortality 18, 74, 121, 131, 169
periods
    missed 19, 136
    see also menstruation
Pfeffer, Naomi and Woollett, Anne 208
Pickard, Barbara 208

Index